History

An Old Testament study of Joshua through Esther

Bob Warren

With grateful hearts we thank:
Jhonda Johnston, editor
Erinn Finley, editor
Jordan Taylor, cover design
Brent Armstrong, executive editor

Copyright © 2004, 2010, 2024 The Hill Publishing/B.A.S.I.C. Training, Inc.
This material may not be reprinted in any form without permission.

ISBN: 978-1-62727-081-6

All Scripture, unless otherwise noted, is from the New American Standard Bible.

Scripture quotations taken from the New American Standard Bible®,
Copyright © 1960, 1962, 1963, 1968, 1971, 1972, 1973,
1975, 1977, 1995 by The Lockman Foundation
Used by permission. (www.Lockman.org)

Table Of Contents

Introduction 3

Week One 5

Week Two 13

Week Three 19

Week Four 27

Week Five 33

Week Six 43

Week Seven 51

Week Eight 61

Week Nine 71

Week Ten 81

Week Eleven 93

Week Twelve 103

Week Thirteen 109

Reference Section 117

Introduction

We are excited that you are giving the Lord an opportunity to build truth into your life. Your fellowship and communion with Him will be greatly enhanced by spending this time in His word.

The "History" section of the Old Testament contains twelve books and covers Israel from their crossing of the Jordan into Canaan, through the judges and the kings, to their exile in Assyria and Babylon, and finally to their return to Canaan from exile in Persia.

The value of knowing the chronology and history of the Jewish people becomes evident when studying the prophets, the gospels, and the rest of the New Testament as well. Reading Scripture about a Jewish Messiah coming to a Jewish nation to fulfill the Jewish Law without the historical context is like eating a plain hotdog while every imaginable condiment is spread out before you. Why settle for plain when you can have amazing?

That's exactly what an understanding of the Pentateuch and History portions of the Old Testament can do for your experience in God's word. That knowledge equips you with compartments of time and context in which to place all the other events in the Bible. What a powerful tool!

The history portion of Scripture is one of the most interesting and essential parts of the Old Testament. Get ready to be blessed! The Lord will take what you learned in the Pentateuch Course and expand your horizons.

If you haven't yet taken the Pentateuch Course, it is recommended as a background before taking the History Course. You can certainly take them in reverse order as long you understand the timeline for both and how they fit together. Please let us know if you need that course.

The History Course is set up as a thirteen-week study with reading and questions to answer each day. The commitment may seem huge at first, but as you adjust to the schedule and realize how much you are learning, it will become a pleasure. Remember, we don't study Scripture to gain knowledge, but to know the heart of the Author. We believe the essence of life for the Christian is to intimately know the heart of our Creator (John 17:3).

When creating our maps, we made every effort to include as many of the place names mentioned in the course. Even with those available it can be difficult to find the places mentioned until you become familiar with many of those locations. To make finding those easier we have included a QR Code to one of our favorite online map resources, bibleatlas.org.

Use your phone or device camera to scan the QR Code image, click the link that shows up and it will take you to the sight. Virtually any place name in Scripture is listed and can be quickly pinpointed. We hope this resource makes your study of the History Course even more fruitful.

Old Testament History　　　　　　**Joshua 1-12**　　　　　　*Week One*

The History Books of the Old Testament

Week One

First Day

Take a few minutes to look over Reference Points 38-60 and familiarize yourself with the other maps and charts of the Reference Section. You will find those resources useful as we take this journey. It will be helpful from the start to know where each is located.

At the end of Deuteronomy, Moses dies (Deuteronomy 34:5) and Joshua is given the responsibility of leading Israel into Canaan. In the book of Joshua, Israel crosses the Jordan and conquers much of Canaan during three military campaigns. By means of these battles the nation learns a very important lesson—that battles are won through God's power and not through superior military strength. Moses had earlier changed Joshua's name from Hoshea, which means "salvation" (Numbers 13:8), to Joshua, which means "Jehovah is Salvation" (Numbers 13:16). He wanted Israel to remember that Jehovah brought victory—not themselves. Therefore, he named their leader "Joshua."

Early in the campaign Israel will learn another important lesson—that sin results in defeat. Victory and sin cannot coexist.

The book of Joshua contains twenty-four chapters, which can be divided as follows:

Chapters 1-12, the first half of the book, give a blow-by-blow account of Israel's battles in Canaan.

Chapters 13-21 describe how the land was divided among the tribes.

Chapter 22 describes the events that surrounded the return of the tribes of Reuben, Gad, and a portion of the tribe of Manasseh to the east side of the Jordan.

Chapters 23-24 record Joshua's farewell addresses as well as the account of his death. The book can be broken down as follows:

A.	Chapters 1-12	Israel takes the land.
B.	Chapters 13-21	Israel divides the land.
C.	Chapter 22	Reuben, Gad, and part of Manasseh return to the conquered territory on the east side of the Jordan.
D.	Chapters 23-24	Joshua instructs Israel to obey God if they desire to remain in the land.

We will seek to accomplish two goals as we study this book: (1) Understanding that faith and obedience bring victory, while unbelief and disobedience result in humiliating defeat. (2) Knowing the geographical territory that each tribe possessed. Being familiar with the layout of the land will be of great value as we study the remaining books of the Old Testament. You will become familiar with many of the names and locations mentioned on the maps included with the course.

During the span of the next six days, you will study the first twelve chapters of Joshua. Next week you will study the last twelve chapters. Enjoy yourself!

The number of people who die at the hands of the Hebrews in the first twelve chapters of Joshua is

Old Testament History *Joshua 1-12* *Week One*

astounding! Is God prejudiced? Does He hate those who are not at peace with His people? Of course not! God knew the Canaanites and the Amorites, along with the other nations in the land, would refuse to worship Him. They, therefore, would serve as a stumbling block to His people. He had them destroyed for this reason. As far back as the time of Abraham, God knew the Amorites would continue to progress in sin (Genesis 15:16). The nations that Israel destroyed had made a choice—to rebel against God to the greatest degree possible. Note: At least their babies would gain access to heaven because of the total annihilation.

Today you will begin covering Reference Point 38, *Joshua Leads Israel into Canaan and Takes Much of the Land*. Israel will now enter the land that was promised to Abraham some 685 years earlier. A large portion of the land will be taken, but not all of it—some will remain under enemy control throughout the remainder of the Old Testament. Israel will not own all the territory promised to her until the Millennial reign of Jesus.

Notice the similarities in Joshua and Jesus. Joshua's name means "God is salvation"—Jesus' name means "Savior." Just as Joshua led the people to victory in Canaan, Jesus leads us to victory today. Pray for wisdom before you start today's questions.

Read Joshua 1, which is associated with Reference Point 38, *Joshua Leads Israel into Canaan and Takes Much of the Land*.

1. Of the promises given to Joshua in verses 3-6, which are the most meaningful to you? Why? From verse 3, did Canaan already belong to the Hebrews, or would it be their possession after they took the land? What does your answer tell you about the certainty of God's promises? Doesn't it make you want to devour God's word?

2. According to verses 7, 8, and 9, what would guarantee success for Joshua and the nation? Memorize verses 8 and 9. Three times the Lord told Joshua to be strong and courageous (vv.6, 7, and 8), for He would be with him (v.9). God was "with" Joshua (v.9) but is "in" those who know Jesus today (Galatians 2:20). When did the Holy Spirit last encourage you to be strong and courageous in Christ's strength?

3. How soon would Israel cross the Jordan (vv.10-11)? What were Reuben, Gad, and the half tribe of Manasseh to do now that Israel was preparing to enter Canaan (vv.12-15)? Review Numbers 32:1-27.

4. What is stated in verses 16-18 that demonstrates the tremendous respect the people had for Joshua? What was the *last* thing they told Joshua in verse 18? When did you last encourage someone in a similar way? Ask the Lord to use your life to encourage those around you.

Read Joshua 2, which is associated with Reference Point 38.

1. The two spies were sent from what location? They were to spy on what city? Who assisted them once they entered the city? What was to be her reward?

Old Testament History *Joshua 1-12* *Week One*

2. Is it important to understand how your enemy perceives God's power (read Joshua 2:8-11)? How is your walk affected when you lose sight of this truth?

3. Rahab and her family were saved by faith in the promise of the spies and the placement of a scarlet thread (v.18). This is a picture of what the blood of Jesus does for mankind—it saves those who receive Christ, from eternal doom. As you complete this study, notice the degree to which the cross is pictured in Old Testament Scripture. Remember also that the Lord used a repentant harlot to accomplish His goals. Therefore, no matter where you have walked or how severely you have failed, repentance allows God to use you in ways that are beyond comprehension. If you were Joshua, how would you have responded after hearing the report of the two spies (v.24)?

Second Day

Read Joshua 3, which is associated with Reference Point 38.

1. When did Joshua arise (v.1)? If you have difficulty completing your daily tasks, you might try rising earlier. Under normal conditions, fewer interruptions occur during the early morning hours. Write down your thoughts below.

2. What was to lead Israel's way as she entered the land? If a cubit equals eighteen inches, how far was this object to proceed in front of Israel (v.4)? (The ark of the covenant was Israel's most treasured possession, for the presence of God dwelt in it.) Why is it imperative that God's presence resides with us while we pass through unfamiliar places (v.4)?

3. To consecrate yourself (v.5) means to lay aside everything that does not glorify God. Why would God require consecration before He would perform wonders among His people (v.5)?

4. What happened when the priests, who carried the ark, stepped into the water? This miracle occurred when the Jordan was at flood stage (v.15). What does this timing say to you about the power of your God? God enjoys coming through when things look the very worst! What hope His power should bring to our souls!

5. Israel entered the land during the time of harvest (v.15). How does their arrival line up with what Jesus stated in Matthew 6:24-34? Do you believe that God can supernaturally meet your material needs? If not, why?

6. According to verse 17, Israel crossed the Jordan on what type of ground? How does this crossing compare with Exodus 14:21-22? Besides allowing Israel passageway into Canaan, what did this supernatural act of God accomplish for Joshua (v.7) and state to the people (v.10)?

Old Testament History **Joshua 1-12** *Week One*

Read Joshua 4, which is associated with Reference Point 38.

1. How many men were to take stones from the Jordan (vv.1-7)? These stones came from what location in the Jordan? What were the men to do with the stones? What purpose would these stones serve? God desired that the future generations of Hebrew children know what had occurred here. How do these instructions tie in with Deuteronomy 6:6-7? We too must teach our children about God's ability to supernaturally provide through the word of God and sharing with them what God has done since coming into our lives!

2. What happened when the priests came up out of the Jordan (v.18)?

3. Who has the responsibility of exalting a man who is in a position of leadership (v.14)? In comparison with the degree to which Israel had trusted Moses, how much would they now trust Joshua (v.14)? Why should the degree of their trust encourage all who are called to lead in the body of Christ?

4. The twelve stones were "set up" at what geographical location (v.20)? Find it on the map titled *Conquest of the Land West of the Jordan*. According to verses 21-24 what was the purpose of these stones? We too must set up stones when God performs the extraordinary in our lives. Recording such events in a journal or diary can accomplish this purpose for us! Those who follow us can then understand, even more deeply, how God has worked in our lives.

Third Day

Read Joshua 5, which is associated with Reference Point 38.

1. Since our enemy knows God's power, how can verse 1 serve as an encouragement when facing life's battles? At this stage, Israel's two major enemies west of the Jordan were the Canaanites and the Amorites, who worshipped several different gods, but mainly Baal. Israel later turned to these gods and was judged for such disobedience.

2. What was done to the sons of Israel in verses 2-8? Why? Although every male who had departed from Egypt had been circumcised, all Hebrew children born in the wilderness remained uncircumcised (vv.5 and 7). Evidently, circumcision had been neglected during the wilderness wanderings because of the sin of the people (v.6).

3. The name "Gilgal" means "rolling." How does this name tie in with what is stated in verse 9? What did Israel observe at Gilgal? This special day on the Jewish calendar was last mentioned in Numbers 9:5. If that was the last time it was officially observed, many years had passed since Israel had celebrated the Passover. Write down your thoughts below.

4. When did the manna cease? How has learning that the Lord allowed Israel to enter the land

Old Testament History **Joshua 1-12** *Week One*

during the time of harvest (Joshua 3:15), increased your appreciation for God's promise in Philippians 4:19?

5. Where was Joshua when his encounter with the captain of the host of the Lord (vv. 13-15), occurred? Much debate exists as to who this being was (some think this was a pre-incarnate appearance of Christ). The thing to digest is that his topic of conversation was holiness. In other words, Israel's leader was to walk in holiness if the nation was to possess the land. Quality leadership is a must if God's people are to consistently overcome the enemy. Write down any new insights below.

Read Joshua 6, which is associated with Reference Point 38.

1. Describe the procedure used in destroying Jericho. What material possessions were spared? What individuals were allowed to live?

2. Describe the curse mentioned in verse 26. Remember this curse, for it will be fulfilled later during the time of the kings. What does verse 27 say about Joshua?

Fourth Day

Read Joshua 7, which is associated with Reference Point 38.

1. Why was Israel defeated at Ai? Read verses 5-9 and try to feel what Joshua and the people must have felt. Write down your thoughts below.

2. When did you last wonder if "crossing the Jordan" (walking in a deeper place of commitment and faith) was worth the cost (v.7)? Do you enjoy living in your comfort zone, or would you rather experience the excitement of having your faith challenged on a regular basis? If you fit the latter category, then God may want to make you into a Joshua! However, on many occasions you will *feel* as Joshua felt in verse 7.

3. How was the problem which brought Israel's defeat at Ai, rectified? What does this correction teach you about God's attitude concerning sin?

Read Joshua 8, which is associated with Reference Point 38.

1. How did the Lord use Israel's defeat at Ai to allow her to eventually overthrow Ai? Think of the times the Lord has used your previous defeats to bring about future victories. Write down any

Old Testament History **Joshua 1-12** **Week One**

comments below. Find Ai on the map *Conquest of the Land West of the Jordan*.

2. What impressed you most about the events of verses 30-35? Find Mount Ebal and Mount Gerizim on the map titled *Conquest of the Land West of the Jordan* (in the Reference Section). Compare what took place here with what was commanded in Deuteronomy 27:2-14.

Fifth Day

Read Joshua 9, which is associated with Reference Point 38.

1. When was the last time your enemies "ganged up" on you (vv.1-2)? How did you respond?

2. Why did the inhabitants of Gibeon desire to make a covenant with Israel? Can you find Gibeon on the map titled *Conquest of the Land West of the Jordan?* Where did they meet with Joshua? Why was it wrong for Israel to enter such a covenant—for assistance read Deuteronomy 20:10-18.

3. According to Joshua 9:14, what caused Israel to read this situation improperly? What does their error teach you about the importance of consulting God before making major decisions? What did Israel do with the inhabitants of Gibeon?

Read Joshua 10, which is associated with Reference Point 38.

Joshua 10 speaks of how Israel took a major portion of the southern region of Canaan.

1. What does verse 2 state about Gibeon? Why did the five kings of the Amorites choose to fight against Gibeon (vv.1-5)? In what cities did these five kings live (v.5)? Find these cities on the map titled *Conquest of the Land West of the Jordan* in the Reference Section.

2. Who rescued the Gibeonites? Through what means did most of the enemy die (v.11)? God took care of Israel although she had disobeyed by entering a covenant with the Gibeonites. However, she did not avoid the consequences (brought about in this life) from her sin (Colossians 3:25).

3. What miracle did God perform at Joshua's request (vv.12-14)? What did Joshua do to the five kings of the Amorites?

4. Verses 28-43 record how Israel took the southern portion of Canaan after destroying the five kings of the Amorites. Record any new insights. According to verse 42, why had Joshua been

Old Testament History   *Joshua 1-12*   Week One

successful in this campaign? To what location did Joshua and Israel return after their battles (v.43)?

Sixth Day

Read Joshua 11, which is associated with Reference Point 38.

Joshua 11 speaks of how Israel took a major portion of the northern region of Canaan.

1. What kings fought against Israel at the waters of Merom? Who won the battle? Find the *3rd Area of Conquest* on the map titled *Conquest of the Land West of the Jordan* in the Reference Section. This territory was conquered by Israel in the campaign—the northern portion of the land. What did Israel do to Hazor, since it was formerly the capital of this region (v.10)? What did Israel do to the remaining cities of these kings? What does the last phrase of verse 15 state about Joshua?

2. On the surface, without the full counsel of God's word, verses 16-23 can appear to say that Israel took the whole land and that every enemy was annihilated (read verse 23). However, many areas had not yet been conquered—read Joshua 13:1. Therefore, the statement in verse 23 about Israel taking the land is a general statement. God had originally promised Moses that Israel would conquer the enemies they faced in battle, and that promise had been fulfilled. Around five years passed while Israel conquered the territory that was now in her possession. Thus, the events of Joshua 6-11 did not take place overnight (read verse 18). Write down any new insights below.

Read Joshua 12, which is associated with Reference Point 38.

1. This chapter lists the territories and cities that Israel conquered on the east and west sides of the Jordan, along with their kings. The names, places, and events mentioned should be somewhat familiar by now. The time you are devoting to God's word is paying huge dividends, so be encouraged. Give yourself a few more weeks and you will be amazed at how much you will have learned. Write down any new insights below. Review the 38 Reference Points you have studied thus far and then write down as many as you can (from memory).

Old Testament History *Joshua 13-24* *Week Two*

The History Books of the Old Testament

Week Two

First Day

Israel controlled Canaan, although much of the land had not yet been conquered. In Joshua 13-21, God divides the land among the tribes—the conquered and unconquered land alike, which meant that each tribe had to continue to trust God if it was to take full possession of its territory. God does a similar thing in our lives today. He places the unconquered territories of our lives before us to teach us to walk by faith.

Over the next few days you will cover Reference Point 39, *Canaan (the Land West of the Jordan) Divided Among 9 1/2 Tribes of Israel—Joshua 13:1-21:45*. Take advantage of the map in the Reference Section titled *The Approximate Territory that the Twelve Tribes Possessed*. It will make your journey much more interesting and allow you to remember the geographical location of each tribe.

Jacob had twelve sons—Reuben, Simeon, Levi, Judah, Issachar, Zebulun, Joseph, Benjamin, Dan, Naphtali, Gad and Asher. Joseph had two sons who received his inheritance (Ephraim and Manasseh). They were adopted by Jacob (Genesis 48:5) and were known as the half-tribe of Ephraim and the half-tribe of Manasseh. Therefore, even though there are thirteen tribal names—Reuben, Simeon, Levi, Judah, Issachar, Zebulun, Ephraim, Manasseh, Benjamin, Dan, Naphtali, Gad and Asher, there are only twelve tribes. Twelve tribal territories (instead of thirteen) are listed on the map *The Approximate Territory that the Twelve Tribes Possessed* because the tribe of Levi received no inheritance in the land (Joshua 13:14). As you read this week's assignment, do not let all the names and places overwhelm you. Just answer the questions included in the course and you will be off and running. Remember—this section is an overview. Have fun and remember to pray for wisdom.

Read Joshua 13, which is associated with Reference Point 39.

1. From what you learned in last week's lesson, along with today's introduction, how are Joshua 13:1 and Joshua 11:23 reconciled? How many tribes were to receive land west of the Jordan (vv.6-7)?

2. Verses 8-33 describe the territories that Reuben, Gad, and the half tribe of Manasseh were to possess east of the Jordan—which had been apportioned to them by Moses (v.32). Refer to the map titled, *The Approximate Territory that the Twelve Tribes Possessed*, and read these verses again. Manasseh was the only tribe to receive territory on both sides of the Jordan. The tribe of Levi received no territorial inheritance (vv.14 and 33). However, they later receive forty-eight cities and their suburbs. Write down any new insights below.

Read Joshua 14, which is associated with Reference Point 39.

1. Who was responsible for dividing the land, and by what means was it divided (vv.1-2)? For more information on who was involved in this process, refer to Numbers 34:16-29.

Old Testament History **Joshua 13-24** **Week Two**

2. What portion of the land did Caleb receive, and why did he receive it? (For more input, read Deuteronomy 1:34-36.) Find this location on the map. How is Caleb described at the end of verses 9 and 14? What is required on our part for similar statements to describe us?

3. How old was Caleb when Moses sent him and the twelve spies into Canaan? How old was Caleb in the present reading? If the Hebrews wandered in the wilderness for forty years, how long had they been in Canaan?

4. Is there any correlation between what is stated about Caleb in verses 9 and 14 and what is stated about him in verse 11? If so, why?

5. Where was Joshua when Caleb approached him concerning his portion of the land? What territory did Caleb desire to possess (vv.12-15)? "Kiriath" (v.15) means "the city of." "Arba" (v.15) "was the greatest man among the Anakim" (v.15), and "the father of Anak" (Joshua 15:13). Thus, Kiriath-arba was the city of the sons of Anak, a city of giants (Numbers 13:33). This territory was also highly fortified and thus more difficult to conquer than other areas of Canaan. What do these conditions tell you about Caleb's character and faith? Are you trusting God to give you the high ground, the harder territories to conquer, or are you satisfied with fighting lesser battles in the lowlands?

Second Day

Read Joshua 15, which is associated with Reference Point 39.

1. A description of Judah's territory is given in Joshua 15, along with more details concerning Caleb's inheritance (vv.13-19). Do not let all the cities, territories, and nations mentioned here intimidate you. Digest what you can and press on. I really mean what I say: PRESS ON! Satan would love to discourage you at this stage of the game. Caleb's inheritance was within the territory allotted to Judah (v.13). (Use the map titled *The Approximate Territory that the Twelve Tribes Possessed.*) Who married Achsah, Caleb's daughter? He was the first judge to rule over Israel (Judges 1:11-15 and Judges 3:9). Record any new insights below.

2. What does verse 63 state about the tribe of Judah? The Jebusites were later driven out by King David (2 Samuel 5:6-10).

Read Joshua 16, which is associated with Reference Point 39.

1. The first four verses of this chapter address the territory allotted to Ephraim and Manasseh. Verses 5-10 give details of the boundaries of the tribe of Ephraim. Ephraim and Manasseh were the sons of what man? Find Ephraim's territory on the map titled *The Approximate Territory that the Twelve Tribes Possessed.* Again, do not become overwhelmed with the names recorded in this chapter. Walk on!

Old Testament History *Joshua 13-24* Week Two

2. What does verse 10 state about the Canaanites? What did the tribe of Ephraim do with them?

Third Day

Read Joshua 17, which is associated with Reference Point 39.

1. This chapter describes the territory allotted to the tribe of Manasseh. Find this territory on the map titled *The Approximate Territory that the Twelve Tribes Possessed,* in the Reference Section. Again, who was Manasseh (v.1)? The territory allotted to the tribe of Manasseh on the west side of the Jordan was allotted to Machir, the firstborn of Manasseh (v.1). The rest of Manasseh's descendants received territory on the east of the Jordan (vv.2-6), ten portions in all (v.5). How do verses 3 and 4 tie in with Numbers 27:1-11? What nation caused a problem for Manasseh? What was done with them?

2. Why did Ephraim and Manasseh desire an additional allotment (v.14)? What did Joshua suggest as a remedy (v.15)? Ephraim and Manasseh demonstrated a lack of faith—not believing they could take their original allotment (v.16). Unlike Caleb, who looked forward to conquering his enemies, Ephraim and Manasseh feared their enemies, the Canaanites. Joshua, being of the tribe of Ephraim, desired that they learn to fight in God's strength and possess their original possession—plus the additional hill country (the forest) he suggested they clear in verse 15 as well as verses 17 and 18. Ephraim and Manasseh failed to drive out their enemies (Judges 1:27). You will be finished with this bombardment of names and places in four more chapters. If you are having difficulty, just remember the general (not detail) location of each tribe. You <u>are</u> growing!

Read Joshua 18, which is associated with Reference Point 39.

1. According to verse 1, what is the name of the new location of Israel's headquarters? The previous location was Gilgal. Find it on the map titled *The Journey of the Ark*. What was set up in Shiloh (v.1)? Shiloh was more centrally located, which made it easier for Israel to worship at the tabernacle. The tabernacle remained at Shiloh for about 300 years.

2. At this time in Israel's history, seven tribes had not yet divided their inheritance on the west side of the Jordan (v.2). The moving of their headquarters from Gilgal to Shiloh had interrupted the partitioning process. Even though the land had previously been divided among the nine and one-half tribes at Gilgal (Joshua 14:1-5), seven of these tribes had to make adjustments due to the territories settled by Judah, Ephraim, and Manasseh. The seven tribes were Benjamin, Simeon, Zebulun, Issachar, Asher, Naphtali, and Dan. What did Joshua require of these seven tribes (vv.4-9)? Remember that the tribe of Levi was not to receive territory as an inheritance, for the priesthood was their inheritance (v.7). Judah and the two half-tribes of Ephraim and Manasseh had received their inheritance west of the Jordan, and Reuben, Gad, and the half-tribe of Manasseh had received theirs east of the Jordan. (Manasseh received territory on both sides of the Jordan.) According to verse 10, how did Joshua respond when they carried out his suggestion?

3. Verses 11-28 describe Benjamin's territory. According to verse 11, where was this territory located? Find it on the map *The Approximate Territory that the Twelve Tribes Possessed*. Familiarize yourself with this location, for many important events are associated with this small

Old Testament History   *Joshua 13-24*   Week Two

piece of real estate. Later in Israel's history, Ephraim and Judah dominated the northern and southern kingdoms (Ephraim to the north and Judah to the south). Benjamin (son of Rachel), Ephraim (grandson of Rachel through Joseph), and Manasseh (grandson of Rachel through Joseph), marched together in the wilderness (Numbers 10:22-24), and were granted territories adjacent to one another. Note too that Judah, their neighbor, was Jacob's son who showed the greatest concern for Benjamin in Genesis 43:8-9 and Genesis 44:18-34. Are you seeing how your study of the Pentateuch makes these Scriptures come alive?

Fourth Day

Read Joshua 19, which is associated with Reference Point 39.

1. Verses 1-9 describe Simeon's allotment. Taking advantage of the map *The Approximate Territory that the Twelve Tribes Possessed,* find this territory. Why was Simeon's territory taken out of Judah's territory (v.9)? Here, God began to fulfill the curse placed on Simeon in Genesis 49:5-7, a curse that resulted from Simeon's evil deeds of Genesis 34:25-30. Simeon was separated from Reuben and Gad, who had received territory on the east side of the Jordan, even though they had marched together in the wilderness (Numbers 10:18-20).

2. Verses 10-48 deal with the allotments of Zebulun, Issachar, Asher, Naphtali, and Dan. Find these areas on the map *The Approximate Territory that the Twelve Tribes Possessed.* What city did Joshua receive? Joshua received his inheritance last. What does his position tell you about his patience and character?

Read Joshua 20, which is associated with Reference Point 39.

1. For more information relating to the cities of refuge, read Numbers 35:6-34 and Deuteronomy 4:41-43 as well as the notes associated with these verses in the Pentateuch study. What was the purpose of a city of refuge? How many cities of refuge were on the east side of the Jordan? How many were located west of the Jordan?

2. Where is your place of refuge? Read Hebrews 4:16 and Psalm 27:5.

Fifth Day

Read Joshua 21, which is the last chapter associated with Reference Point 39.

1. What did the leaders of the tribe of Levi request of Eleazar the priest, Joshua, and the leaders of the tribes of Israel (vv.1-2)? On what grounds could they make this request (v.3; Numbers 35:2)?

The following list should assist you in understanding how these cities were divided.

Sons of Kohath: 23 cities

Old Testament History *Joshua 13-24* **Week Two**

Sons of Gershon: 13 cities
Sons of Merari: <u>12</u> cities
Total number of Levitical cities: 48

Aaron's sons, who served as priests, received thirteen Levitical cities from the tribes of Judah, Simeon, and Benjamin (v.4). The remaining Levites received thirty-five cities from the other tribes, totaling forty-eight Levitical cities in all. These cities were located on both sides of the Jordan; six were cities of refuge.

2. What do verses 43-45 communicate about God's ability to fulfill His promises? The land was now at rest, but the Hebrews had yet to take much of it (God had promised that Israel's enemies would be driven out gradually rather than all at once—Exodus 23:29-30.) Therefore, God had fulfilled His promise of giving Israel the land (in a general sense) even though much of the land remained in enemy hands. Joshua 23:1-13 confirms this fact. Reuben, Gad, and the half tribe of Manasseh were set to return to their territory east of the Jordan. You have completed your study of Reference Point 39.

Sixth Day

Joshua 22:1-24:33 falls between Reference Points 39 and 40. An overview of this section of Scripture follows. Feel free to read these verses in your Bible if time permits.

Joshua 22 Now that Israel controlled much of Canaan, Joshua sent Reuben, Gad, and Manasseh to their tents on the east side of the Jordan (vv.1-9). These tribes had fulfilled their promise of Numbers 32:16-32. However, as they returned home, they built an altar on the west side of the Jordan (v.10), which was a copy of the altar of the Lord (v.28). This act angered the other tribes until they discovered its purpose (vv.11-34). It was a memorial—not an altar built for burnt offering or sacrifice. Reuben, Gad, and Manasseh desired that Israel continually view the eastern tribes as part of God's possession. They wanted all the Hebrew offspring to know that the tribes living on the east side of the Jordan worshipped the same God. Thus, they built the memorial and named it *Witness* (v.34). All tribes were to gather three times each year in only one place—before the Lord at the tabernacle (Exodus 23:17), which was, at this time, located at Shiloh.

This account confirms the importance of gathering all the facts before drawing final conclusions. Many innocent victims would have lost their lives had Israel failed to send Phinehas and his delegation to communicate with the three tribes returning to the east of the Jordan.

Joshua 23 Several years elapsed between Joshua's apportioning the land and the events recorded in this chapter (v.1). Joshua's farewell address (probably given at Shiloh) is recorded here, along with a strong exhortation for the nation to walk in obedience (vv.2-16). Joshua directed these statements to the leaders of the nation (v.2), while in the next chapter he addresses the entire nation. He wanted to make sure that Israel did not fall into complacency and fail to allow God to drive out her enemies (vv.3-13).

Joshua was a wonderful leader, but he neglected to consistently pour his life into men who could lead after his departure. Yes, the elders *watched* as Joshua led the nation, but they were not discipled (instructed on a consistent basis) to the degree that Joshua had been discipled (instructed) by Moses. This problem becomes very evident in the next chapter. I believe he realized his error and, here, tried to cover for his mistake. But it was too little too late. The book of Judges illustrates how much his error, and the corresponding lack of leadership, affected the nation.

Old Testament History   **Joshua 13-24**   *Week Two*

After addressing God's faithfulness (v.14), Joshua revealed the ramifications of Israel's future disobedience (vv.15-16). Israel would worship the gods of the nations and perish from the land (vv.15-16). It must have broken Joshua's heart to know that those he had served would soon disobey. But capable leadership is a necessity if a people are to live uncompromisingly. If only Joshua had consistently poured his life into just one man (as Moses had done with him)!

<u>Joshua 24</u> Joshua continued his farewell addresses, only this time at Shechem (v.1). After reviewing the history of the nation (vv.2-13), he encouraged the people to choose whom they would serve (vv.14-15). They agreed to serve the Lord (vv.16-24), after which Joshua made a covenant with the people (v.25). This covenant was final and binding, for Joshua wrote the words of the covenant in the book of the law (v.26)—the book of the law that Moses had placed beside the ark of the covenant in Deuteronomy 31:24-27. He also set up a large stone "under the oak that was by the sanctuary of the Lord" (v.26)—possibly the same location mentioned in Genesis 12:6, where Abraham had built an altar and worshipped the Lord, and where Jacob had cleansed his household from foreign gods, which he buried under this same tree (Genesis 35:2,4). The stone would serve as a witness to the fact that Israel had entered the covenant (v.27). Consequently, Israel would reap God's blessings for obedience and curses for disobedience. Joshua then died at the age of one hundred and ten (v.29) and was buried "in the territory of his inheritance in Timnath-serah" (v.30). "Israel served the Lord all the days of Joshua and all the days of the elders who survived Joshua" (v.31). Israel obeyed for such a short time span because the elders who followed Joshua were ill equipped to disciple future leaders. Joshua had failed to teach them how to do so.

Verse 32 states that Joseph's bones were buried at Shechem—even though this may have occurred much earlier. This burial fulfilled Joseph's request of Genesis 50:25-26. Eleazar, the high priest, the son of Aaron also died (v.33). Eleazar's son, Phinehas, served as high priest in his place (v.33).

You are growing! Enjoy your day off tomorrow and do something to reward yourself for continuing your study of God's word (like going to Dairy Queen and indulging in a Blizzard—or even a Breeze, which is a low-fat Blizzard). Remember, it is spiritual to laugh and have a good time in our Lord (and even eat ice cream if done in moderation)! You need to review the reference points that you have studied up to now, so squeeze that in before you close your workbook.

Old Testament History   *Judges 1-12*   *Week Three*

The History Books of the Old Testament

Week Three

First Day

This week you will study the first twelve chapters of the book of Judges. Judges, describing the events surrounding the twelve judges who ruled over God's people, covers Israel's history between Joshua's death and the arrival of Samuel in the book of First Samuel. (Samuel was a judge as well, and we can view him as Israel's last judge since his sons, who followed him, were ineffective—1 Samuel 8:1-3.) The book of Ruth, which follows Judges and precedes First Samuel, records events that occurred during the time of Judges.

Israel needed strong leadership to replace Joshua if they were to remain in the land. God used twelve judges to deliver His people, each judge being used of Jehovah to eliminate a particular crisis. In almost every instance, the rulership of a particular judge followed a time of gross disobedience within the nation. When Israel disobeyed, God would raise up an enemy, Israel would repent, God would raise up a judge, and the judge would be used to deliver the people. Israel would then temporarily walk in obedience, fall into disobedience, and the whole cycle would replay itself.

Some of the judges ruled at the same time, which makes the chronology of the judges uncertain. However, it is widely accepted that the book of Judges spans around 325 years.

This book makes two things very clear. Sin results in spiritual blindness, whereas repentance brings God's blessing and favor. Regardless of the depth of Israel's sin, she was delivered each time she repented—confirming that we serve a loving and forgiving God. Judges proves this point as well as any book in the Old Testament. But don't think for one second that Israel failed to reap consequences from her sin. Even though God delivered her time and time again, her sin kept her from maturing in her walk with God. Her disobedience eventually resulted in exile from Canaan (which is detailed in Second Kings).

Reference Point 40 is associated with the entire book of Judges. This book contains names and geographical locations that may be foreign to you. Don't be concerned. You will be fine. Just remember to pray for wisdom and walk on!

In the book of Joshua, Israel conquered much of Canaan while fighting as a unit. In the book of Judges, the tribes separate and attempt to take the land that remained in their individual tribal territories.

Read Judges 1, which is associated with Reference Point 40, *Judges Rule After Joshua, Judges 1:1-21:25.*

Use the map titled *The Approximate Territory that the Twelve Tribes Possessed* (in the Reference Section) along with the other materials available.

1. Which tribe went up first against the Canaanites? Who went with them? Why? (Tie Joshua 19:9 into these verses.) How much success did they have? What major city did Judah capture in verse 8? (Even though Jerusalem was temporarily overthrown, it was not a permanent possession of Israel until King David's day—2 Samuel 5:6-9.)

Old Testament History   **Judges 1-12**   *Week Three*

2. After conquering Jerusalem, Judah traveled south to fight against the Canaanites. The events recorded in verses 10-15 are also recorded in Joshua 15:13-19. What two cities did Judah take in verses 10-15 (Sheshai, Ahiman, and Talmai were the three sons of Anak—Joshua 15:14)? From previous studies, why was Hebron given to Caleb? (You might want to review your notes on Joshua 14 and 15.) How was Othniel related to Caleb? What city did he take? What reward did he receive for taking the city?

3. What territories did Judah and Simeon take in verses 17 and 18? Can you find them on the map? Why did Judah have difficulty driving out the enemies in the valleys (v.19)? Verse 20 simply restates Caleb's conquest of Hebron.

4. With whom did the tribe of Benjamin struggle in Jerusalem (v.21)? This conflict confirms that even though Judah took the city in verse 8, it was not held permanently. (Remember that Jerusalem was within Benjamin's territory.) What nation presented a problem for Manasseh, Ephraim, Zebulun, Asher, and Naphtali? What nation presented a problem for the tribe of Dan?

5. God had promised that no nation could stand against His people so long as they walked in faith and obedience. Israel was not walking in faith and obedience. From where does faith come (read Romans 10:17)? Could our lack of faith result from a lack of revelation of the truth? Need I say more about the importance of knowing truth?

Second Day

Read Judges 2, which is associated with Reference Point 40.

1. According to verses 1-3, why would God cease driving out Israel's enemies? Israel had disobeyed the Lord which set the stage for the book of Judges, for God will raise up enemies to force Israel back to Himself. How did Israel respond to God's words (v.4)?

2. According to verses 6-10, how long did Israel serve the Lord? What does their inconsistency tell you about the importance of strong, godly leadership? How does it tie in with Paul's words to Timothy in 2 Timothy 2:2? What is stated about the generation that lived after Joshua and the elders who survived Joshua (v.10)? Do you desire to teach the truths you are learning to faithful men and women?

3. Verses 11-23 relate a series of events repeated over and over in the book of Judges. What occurred here? Also tie these events into the second paragraph of this week's introduction. When was the last time the Lord raised up a problem for the sole purpose of getting you back on track?

Read Judges 3, which is associated with Reference Point 40.

Old Testament History **Judges 1-12** *Week Three*

1. Why did the Lord leave some of Israel's enemies in the land (vv.1-2, 4)? What enemies did the Lord leave in the land (v.3)? What enemy is the Lord using in your life to teach you how to war with spiritual weaponry?

2. What did Israel do that caused the Lord to raise up an enemy (vv.5-7)? Who was that enemy? What judge defeated this enemy? How long did the land have rest?

As you work through Judges, you should complete the chart titled *The Judges of Israel* (located in the Reference Section). The chart deals with the following categories:

(a)   The judge that God raised up
(b)   Tribe to which the judge belonged
(c)   Israel's sin
(d)   The enemy that God raised up
(e)   The length of time the enemy suppressed Israel
(f)   The length of time the land had peace
(g)   Judges' Scripture references

You will be unable to complete every category of the chart since sufficient information to do so is not recorded in Scripture. But fill in what you can. A completed chart of the judges is also supplied in the Reference Section. Feel free to use it to check your work. Also take advantage of the maps supplied in the reference section.

3. Read verses 12-30 and continue to complete the chart of the judges. From verse 19, would you say that Jehovah continued to be worshipped at Gilgal (if, indeed, this "Gilgal" is the same one where Israel first camped when she entered Canaan—Joshua 4:19-20; 5:9-10)? Can you remember where Moab was located? Verse 31 mentions another judge. Record the information concerning this judge on the chart. Only one other judge will deliver Israel from the Philistines in the book of Judges. His name is Samson, and we will look at his life in chapters 13-16.

Third Day

Read Judges 4, which is associated with Reference Point 40.

Use the *General Map of Israel* to get your bearings (remember names like Mt. Tabor, the Kishon River, Ramah, and E—they are important locations in the Old Testament).

1. This chapter is about Deborah, the next judge of Israel. Take the information given here and fill in the chart titled *The Judges of Israel*. Considering the map titled *The Approximate Territory that the Twelve Tribes Possessed* and *General Map of Israel* (in the Reference Section), along with the location of the battle and Barak's place of residence (Kedesh-naphtali), why would Deborah suggest that Barak choose men from the tribes of Naphtali and Zebulun to fight alongside him (v.6)? (These weren't the only tribes that assisted in the battle—read Judges 5:14-15, the next chapter we will study.) Knowing the tribal territories adds richness to God's word.

Old Testament History   **Judges 1-12**   *Week Three*

2. Who killed Sisera, the commander of Jabin's army? According to verses 11 and 17, Sisera's killer had family ties with Moses. How? In your opinion, was Barak a man of faith? What does God think of him (read Hebrews 11:32-34)? Why should it encourage you to know that God perceives Barak as such, even though he had major weaknesses?

Read Judges 5, which is associated with Reference Point 40.

1. Who wrote this song? Verse 8 reveals why God raised up the problem with Jabin king of Canaan, who reigned in Hazor. What was the reason (notice the small "g" is used in association with "gods" in this verse)? Which statement in this chapter spoke to you the most? Try to imagine the joy that Deborah, Barak, and the people of Israel enjoyed at this time.

Fourth Day

Judges 6-8 tells of Gideon, a very famous Old Testament judge. As you read these chapters, record the proper information on the chart titled *The Judges of Israel*. Also follow the action on the maps included in the Reference Section. By realizing which tribe Gideon was from, and by using the maps, you will see why certain tribes and cities are mentioned. Buckle up! We are going to cover the entire account of Gideon (Judges 6-8). All three chapters are associated with Reference Point 40.

Read Judges 6, which is associated with Reference Point 40.

1. Why did God raise up an enemy? Who was Israel's enemy? The lineage of this enemy can be traced back to Keturah, Abraham's concubine (Genesis 25:1-2). What did Israel do as a result of her predicament (v.6)? When did you last feel as Gideon felt in verse 13? How would the events of verses 14-24 have encouraged you to pursue God's purpose for your life?

2. Why should verses 25-32 encourage you to live a life of no compromise, even around your own family members?

3. What three signs did God perform to reassure Gideon of victory (vv.21, 38, 40)? Do you always need a "sign" to carry out God's will? We must never forget that the word of God is our main resource when determining God's will. If a "sign" should contradict what the word says, we must forget the "sign." To which tribe did Gideon belong (v.15)? From looking at the map titled *The Approximate Territory that the Twelve Tribes Possessed,* and knowing where Gideon was from, can you understand why he would send for help from Manasseh, Asher, Zebulun, and Naphtali (v.35)?

Read Judges 7, which is associated with Reference Point 40.

Record the required information on the chart of the judges. Also follow the action on the maps.

Old Testament History   *Judges 1-12*   Week Three

1. What did you learn from the incident recorded in verses 1-8? How would you have responded if you were Gideon?

2. From verses 9-15, how did God further confirm to Gideon that he would prevail over the Midianites?

3. According to verse 22, how were the Midianites defeated? Can God cause the same thing to happen to our enemies? What were the names of the two leaders of Midian, and what tribe was responsible for their death (vv.24-25)?

Read Judges 8, which is associated with Reference Point 40.

Take the information from this chapter and fill in the chart of the judges. Also follow on the maps.

1. Why was the tribe of Ephraim so upset (v.1)? What impressed you about Gideon's response (vv.2-3)? Do you see wisdom at work here? Explain.

2. How are Gideon and his men described in verse 4? When did you last find yourself "weary yet pursuing"? What did you learn about yourself and about your God from the situation?

3. Use the map in the reference section to follow Gideon's pursuit of Zebah and Zalmunna, kings of Midian (vv.5-21). What impressed you about Gideon in verses 22-23?

4. Can a man of God make a poor choice? What did Gideon do in verses 24-27 that was not wise? The exact nature of this ephod is difficult to determine. An ephod was part of the priest's attire (Exodus 28:4), and on occasion it was consulted for divine guidance (1 Samuel 23:9-12). What do you learn from the fact that Gideon's ephod made Israel stumble? We too, like Gideon, become more vulnerable to deception after a great spiritual victory. Therefore, we must continually remain alert!

5. Jerubbaal was Gideon (v.29). Gideon's wives bore him how many sons (v.30)? His concubine in Shechem bore him what son (v.31)? What did Israel do after Gideon's death (vv.33-35)? What do these actions tell you about the importance of godly leadership?

Fifth Day

Read Judges 9, which is associated with Reference Point 40.

1. Use the map titled *The Approximate Territory that the Twelve Tribes Possessed* (in the Reference

Old Testament History   ***Judges 1-12***   ***Week Three***

Section). Where did Abimelech go, and what did he do in verses 1-2? Remember that Abimelech was the son of Gideon's concubine at Shechem. How did the leaders of Shechem respond to Abimelech's idea (v.3)? According to verse 4, from what resource did Abimelech receive financial support and whom did he hire to assist him? What did Abimelech do to the seventy sons of Gideon? Where did he do it? Which son of Gideon escaped?

2. What did the leaders of Shechem do to Abimelech according to verse 6? Where did they do it (v.6)? What else had occurred at this location since Israel's return to Canaan (Joshua 24:25-27)? Shechem is located near Mt. Gerizim. Can you now understand how Jotham could stand on Mt. Gerizim and speak to the people of Shechem? What impressed you the most about Jotham's speech (vv.7-20)?

3. How long did Abimelech rule over Israel? What did God do to sever the relationship between Abimelech and the men of Shechem (vv.23-24)? Isn't it encouraging to know that God can do similar things to bring about justice in our land? How was Gaal used to bring further dissension between Abimelech and the people of Shechem (vv.26-41)? Abimelech dwelt in Arumah (v.41), not Shechem.

4. What did Abimelech eventually do to Shechem in verses 45 and 49? According to verses 53 and 54, how did Abimelech die? What do verses 56-57 state about God?

Read Judges 10, which is associated with Reference Point 40.

1. Use the map titled *The Approximate Territory that the Twelve Tribes Possessed,* as you work through today's questions. Two judges, Tola and Jair, are mentioned in verses 1-5. To which tribe did Tola belong? How long did he judge Israel? From where was Jair? To which tribe did Jair belong (Numbers 32:40-41)? How long did Jair judge Israel? Take the information in verses 1-5 and fill in the chart of the judges.

2. Israel again turned against the Lord (vv.6-9). What enemies did God raise up in response to Israel's disobedience? (The Philistines are not dealt with specifically until Judges 13—during Samson's day.) According to verses 8, how long and in what geographical location did Ammon afflict Israel? From our study of the Pentateuch (the first five books of the Old Testament), where did the sons of Ammon live, and how did they come into existence? What other tribes did Ammon eventually afflict (v.9)?

3. What do verses 10-16 (especially verse 16) tell you about God's mercy and compassion? For whom was Israel looking at the end of this chapter?

Old Testament History   *Judges 1-12*   *Week Three*

Sixth Day

Read Judges 11, which is associated with Reference Point 40.

Take what you learned yesterday in Judges 10:6-18, tie it in with what happened with Jephthah, and continue to fill in the chart of the judges. Most of the action of this chapter takes place on the east side of the Jordan.

1. Why did Jephthah leave his homeland? Where did he go? (This location was probably northeast of Gilead since the people of Tob joined the Ammonites and fought against David in 2 Samuel 10:6-8.) Who asked him to return to Gilead? What position of authority did Jephthah hold when he returned? How can this turn of events in Jephthah's life serve to encourage us?

2. The information in verses 12-26 should be very familiar from our previous study of the Pentateuch (the first five books of the Old Testament). According to these verses, why did Israel have a legitimate right to possess the land of Gilead? How did the king of Ammon respond to Jephthah's messages?

3. Describe the vow that Jephthah made to the Lord (vv.29-31). What resulted? Is your word your bond? When was the last time you promised to do something and fulfilled your promise out of raw obedience (with no feelings attached)? Note: Some people think that Jephthah, being raised with heathen ideas, sacrificed his daughter to fulfill his vow. Others think the vow was fulfilled through the daughter remaining a virgin until death.

Read Judges 12, which is associated with Reference Point 40.

1. What was Ephraim complaining about this time? What did it cost them? What does this situation communicate about the cost of jealousy and strife? Both Ephraim and Jephthah responded improperly here. Ephraim was jealous over, "not being invited to fight against Ammon" (v.1)—even though Jephthah evidently invited them (v.2). Jephthah's retaliation was wrong in that two wrongs never make a right. This whole problem could have been avoided had both sides been willing to work out their differences. As a result of Jephthah's impulsiveness, many in Israel lost their lives.

Old Testament History   ***Judges 1-12***   ***Week Three***

2. Record the information pertaining to Jephthah on the chart of the judges. This chapter covers three more judges who ruled over Israel: Ibzan, Elon, and Abdon. Record this information in the chart of the judges.

Look over the chart of the judges. Aren't you encouraged with what you are learning? Just wait until next week when we study the life of Samson! If time allows, try to review all the Reference Points you have studied thus far. You are doing great!

Old Testament History *Judges 13-21; Ruth 1-4* *Week Four*

The History Books of the Old Testament

Week Four

First Day

Today you will begin reading about Samson, one of the most famous judges in the Old Testament. Pray for wisdom each day before doing your assignment. Also fill in the appropriate information relating to Samson on the chart of the judges.

Read Judges 13, which is associated with Reference Point 40.

1. What does verse 1 state about Israel? What did the Lord do as a result of Israel's sin (v.1)? From what tribe was Samson (v.2)? What do verses 5 and 7 state about Samson? Read Numbers 6:2-5 to find out more about the Nazirite vow, and record anything that catches your attention. Samson would fight against the Philistines and *begin* to deliver Israel (even though Israel would not be fully delivered from the Philistines until King David's day). The Philistines lived on the coast of the Mediterranean Sea in such areas as Gaza, Ekron, and Gath. Go to the map entitled *The Approximate Territory that the Twelve Tribes Possessed* (use the *General Map of Israel* as well) and notice how close the territory of Dan was located to Philistine territory, which explains why the Lord would choose a man from the tribe of Dan to fight against the Philistines.

2. What did you learn from the angel's encounter with Manoah and his wife?

3. What does the statement, "the Spirit of the Lord began to stir him" (v.25) mean to you? When did this last happen to you, and what did He "stir" within you?

Read Judges 14, which is associated with Reference Point 40.

1. According to verses 1 and 2, what was in Timnah that Samson desired? Why did he want her (v.3)? Does this story tell you anything about Samson's level of maturity? Explain. Why did the Lord "allow" this union to take place (v.4)?

2. How did the Lord use Samson's marriage to begin to bring destruction within the Philistine nation? To whom was Samson's wife given?

Old Testament History   *Judges 13-21; Ruth 1-4*   *Week Four*

3. How does this chapter confirm that a believer should not marry a non-believer (2 Cor. 6:14)?

Second Day

Read Judges 15, which is associated with Reference Point 40.

1. What did Samson do after discovering that his wife had been given to his friend? What happened to Samson's wife and father-in-law due to these events? What did Samson then do to the Philistines?

2. According to verses 9-19, what occurred when the Philistines came to Judah to seize Samson? How many Philistines did Samson kill, and how did he kill them?

3. How long did Samson judge Israel? Write down the main thing you learned from this chapter. How can this account help you in your walk with Christ?

Read Judges 16, which is associated with Reference Point 40.

1. What did Samson see in Gaza that eventually brought him trouble? Who did he see in the valley of Sorek that brought him even more trouble? What was Samson's major weakness? Sin can blind. What is your greatest area of weakness? What are you doing to allow God to deliver you?

2. Does it concern you that a person who knows the Lord (and possesses supernatural strength) can so suddenly lose it? How does this situation serve as a warning to you in the spiritual realm?

3. What impressed you about the manner in which Samson died? Take the information from the life of Samson and fill in the chart of the judges.

Old Testament History   *Judges 13-21; Ruth 1-4*   *Week Four*

Third Day

Our next section of Scripture deals with the tribe of Dan and how they established the city of Dan. Judges 17:1-18:31 tells about Micah. He built an ungodly place of worship (which shows that he had a zeal for God but not according to knowledge). He also hired a Levite (a misguided Levite at that) to serve as his priest. When the Danites moved north to take the city of Laish, they stole Micah's household idols, along with his priest, and established a false place of worship. The Danites were originally given territory adjacent to Benjamin and Ephraim (look at the map titled *The Approximate Territory that the Twelve Tribes Possessed*). However, because of their lack of faith, they were unable to drive out the Amorites (Judges 1:34). They then decided to go north. When they did, they established a false place of worship in the northern portion of Canaan, a place that would be a thorn in the side of Israel for years to come.

Read Judges 17, which is associated with Reference Point 40.

1. What occurred that caused Micah to possess a graven image and a molten image? Who served as his first priest? Who replaced this priest, and where was he from?

2. After studying this chapter (especially verse 6), how would you describe Israel's spiritual condition? Could Romans 10:2 describe her state? What similarities do you see in what occurred here and the spiritual condition of our nation today? You will see the fruit of Israel's sin in the next few chapters. What you study will not be pretty!

Read Judges 18, which is associated with Reference Point 40.

1. The Danites had been assigned territory in Canaan (Joshua 19:40-48). However, they failed to drive out the Amorites and were cramped for space (Judges 1:34)—thus the statement in Judges 18:1. How many spies were sent from Dan to find new territory? Where did they lodge first? What did they ask of Micah's priest (vv.3-5), and how did he respond (v.6)? Do the spies' questions tell you anything about their inability to discern "true religion" from "false religion"? If so, what? The spies may have known this priest previously (v.3).

2. What city did the spies choose, and why (vv.7, 9-10)? People who walk outside God's will desire the path of least resistance. After all, to take the land originally allotted would require a battle fought in faith. To take Laish would be a cakewalk. When was the last time you disobeyed and took the path of least resistance? What resulted? The remainder of the Old Testament will confirm the great price the Danites paid for their lack of faith.

3. Was Micah's priest loyal or disloyal to him? What do the priest's actions tell you about the stability of relationships based on things other than truth from God's word?

Old Testament History   *Judges 13-21; Ruth 1-4*   *Week Four*

4. According to the statement, "and what do I have besides" (v.24), Micah had put all his eggs in one basket. Is there anything in your life that you could not live without? If so, what is it? The Lord wants you to worship Him and Him alone!

5. What did the tribe of Dan do to the inhabitants of Laish as well as the city? What did they name the city after rebuilding it? What did they do with Micah's graven image? Who was their priest? During the time of the kings this territory will be used to establish another form of false worship in Israel. Note: "Jonathan, the son of Gershom, the son of Manasseh" (v.30) is an interesting person, especially when considering that "Manasseh," according to some of the ancient versions of the Scriptures, may very well have been Moses. If this lineage is the case, then Jonathan was a direct descendant of the man who led Israel out of Egypt, again displaying the downward spiral of spirituality within the nation.

Fourth Day

Judges 19:1-21:25 tells one of the saddest stories in the entire word of God. A concubine of a Levite was physically abused (to the point of death) by a group of men from the city of Gibeah (which was within the territory of Benjamin). Also, these Benjamites first desired to perform homosexual acts with her husband, the Levite. The tribe of Benjamin was never the same after this incident. In fact, Saul states later that his tribe, the tribe of Benjamin, was the smallest in Israel (1 Samuel 9:21).

Read Judges 19:1 - 21:25, which is associated with Reference Point 40.

1. What did you learn from these chapters about the cost of sin?

2. As you read today's assignment, what did you learn about the grace of God?

3. Why should today's lesson encourage you to take a stronger stand against sin in your community?

You have now finished the book of Judges. You should have completed the chart of the judges, a chart you can review anytime you need to survey the book. You are doing great! God will greatly honor the time you are giving Him in His word!

Old Testament History   *Judges 13-21; Ruth 1-4*   **Week Four**

Fifth Day

Because the events recorded in the book of Ruth occurred during the time of the judges, we will cover this book next. We will only do an overview since no judge is mentioned. This book addresses the life of Ruth (a Moabite), who married Boaz (a Jew), and became the great-grandmother of King David.

Ruth 1 The events recorded in the book of Ruth occurred during the time of the judges (v.1). Because of a famine in the land, Elimelech, of the tribe of Judah, and Naomi (his wife), along with their two sons (Mahlon and Chilion), moved to Moab (vv.1-2). While in Moab, Elimelech died (v.3). Mahlon and Chilion then married two Moabite women named Orpah and Ruth (v.4), after which both sons died (v.5). Many ancient Jews believed that Elimelech, Mahlon, and Chilion all died because of disobedience. They viewed Elimelech as walking out of God's will by leaving Canaan and moving to Moab. They argued that God would have met his needs even in the midst of the famine. They also argued that Mahlon and Chilion sinned by marrying Moabite women (Deuteronomy 23:3), and thus paid for their sin with their lives. However, God uses these events to make way for the Messiah. God truly is sovereign. No book in His word confirms His sovereignty more profoundly than the book of Ruth.

The famine in Canaan subsided (v.6), so Naomi desired to return to her homeland (vv.6-7). After Naomi encouraged Orpah and Ruth to remain in Moab (vv.8-14), Orpah remained (v.15), but Ruth clung to Naomi (v.14). Ruth even made Naomi's people and God her very own (vv.16-17)—she forsook the Moabites and the Moabite gods. In other words, she considered herself to be Jewish. Naomi and Ruth traveled to Bethlehem; the entire city heard of their arrival which was during the barley festival (vv.18-22).

Ruth 2 As God would have it (since He is sovereign), Ruth gleaned barley in a field owned by Boaz, Elimelech's relative or "kinsman" (vv.1-3). Upon returning from Bethlehem (v.4), Boaz discovered Ruth (vv.5-7) and insisted that she remain in his fields (vv.8-9). Boaz showed favor toward Ruth because of Ruth's faithfulness to Naomi (vv.10-13). He even had his reapers purposely pull grain from the bundles for Ruth to glean (vv.14-16). Isn't it amazing how God cares for the faithful? Ruth returned to Naomi (with the grain) and related what had transpired (vv.17-19). Naomi, surprised (and very excited) over these events, told Ruth that Boaz was one of their closest relatives (v.20). Ruth gleaned in Boaz's fields until the end of the barley and wheat harvests and continued to live with Naomi (vv.21-23).

Sixth Day

Ruth 3 Since Boaz was a close relative, Naomi sought security for Ruth by having her sleep at Boaz's feet (vv.1-9). (Naomi uses the phrase "our kinsman" in verse 2. Since Ruth had forsaken her Moabite ancestry and become a Jew, and since Boaz was Naomi's close relative, Naomi's statement here is proper and valid.) The Law made provisions for childless widows. The widow's brother-in-law was to marry her and name their first-born after the deceased husband (Deuteronomy 25:5-6). This requirement was to preserve the deceased husband's name in Israel (Deuteronomy 25:6). Boaz was not Ruth's brother-in-law, but he was a "kinsman" (v.2), and Ruth had no children. Apparently, it was the custom (in abnormal situations), for children to be borne by close relatives even before the Law was instituted (Genesis 38—Judah and Tamar—which is referenced in Ruth 4:12).

Boaz and all of Bethlehem understood that Ruth was a woman of excellence (vv.10-11). And guess what? Such women make wonderful wives. It is no surprise that Boaz desired to "redeem" (marry) Ruth. However, a relative (kinsman) closer to Ruth than Boaz (v.12) stood in the way. Boaz would now visit this man to see if he desired to marry Ruth (v.13). The chapter ends with Ruth returning to Naomi awaiting news from Boaz (vv.14-18). From the last phrase in verse 18, Boaz was a man of diligence, a trustworthy man, a man who could apply himself to a matter and see it through. Oh, how the world needs such men!

Ruth 4 Only after the kinsman refused to redeem Ruth (vv.1-8) did Boaz pursue her (vv.9-10). What character and integrity Boaz possessed! The leaders of the city even placed a blessing upon the union between Boaz and Ruth (vv.11-12). Ruth and Boaz married and had a son (v.13). His name was Obed, and his grandson would be King David (vv.13-22). God used Naomi's "negative circumstances" for good.

Boaz's relationship with Ruth points to Christ's relationship with the church. Boaz (a Jew) had no reason to show favor toward Ruth (a Gentile). Neither did Jesus (a Jew) have any reason to show favor toward Gentiles. However, Leviticus 25:25 gives information relating to the kinsman redeemer. If a Jew lost his material possessions, his creditors could make him their slave. His nearest of kin, however, if he desired to do so, could pay the debt and secure his relative's freedom. This tradition is why Jesus had to come as a descendant of Abraham. The Jews were given the Law but could not keep the Law (Galatians 3:24; Romans 3:20). Their sin held them in bondage (John 8:34), but Jesus held the price of redemption. His innocent blood paid the debt in full (1 Peter 1:18-19). Through faith in Christ, a Jew is released from his bondage to enjoy all the benefits of being a member of God's family. Through faith in Christ, Gentiles become *spiritual* descendants of Abraham (Galatians 3:29). Like Israel, we had a sin debt we could not pay. Jesus, our brother through faith, became a man, paid our sin debt, and set us free. Also, as was necessary of the kinsman redeemer, Jesus had to desire to pay the redemption price. Because John 10:18 states that Jesus laid down His life freely, we know that He endured the cross voluntarily. Isn't He a wonderful Savior?! Doesn't this knowledge make you want to know as much about Him as you possibly can? Thus, Jesus became a Jew to fulfill a very special office—that of kinsman redeemer.

Enjoy your day off tomorrow. Take a walk with the Lord (just you and Him) and tell Him what a great God He is. Also spend part of that time in silence before Him—just listening. If He isn't already, He can become the best Friend you have!

Old Testament History *1 Samuel 1-19* *Week Five*

The History Books of the Old Testament

Week Five

First Day

The book of First Samuel contains the account of Samuel, the last honorable Old Testament judge. His parents resided in the hill country of Ephraim (Ramah to be exact), and after visiting Shiloh to worship (the ark of the covenant was moved to Shiloh in Joshua 18:1), Hannah (Samuel's mother) conceived and gave birth to Samuel.

This book records Samuel's stay with Eli the high priest, who also served as judge. Eli, a descendant of Ithamar, the younger son of Aaron (Exodus 28:1), served as high priest instead of a descendant of Eleazar, Aaron's older son, who was high priest in Joshua's day (Joshua 24:33). (We can know that Eli was of Ithamar's lineage because 1 Chronicles 24:3 states that Ahimelech, a descendant of Eli (1Kings 2:27), was a descendant of Ithamar.) The priesthood is restored to the family of Eleazar when King Solomon appoints Zadok priest (1 Kings 2:35).

Samuel matured even though Eli failed to meet the spiritual needs of his family and nation. The Philistines played havoc with Israel during this time, and eventually took the ark of the covenant into Philistine territory.

This book also records Samuel's experiences with King Saul, the first king of Israel. Even though Saul reigned, David captured the hearts of the people. Therefore, much of First Samuel deals with Saul's overwhelming passion to destroy David. It also records David's godly responses to Saul's assaults. David does not reign until Second Samuel, but Samuel anointed him as king even while Saul reigned (1 Samuel 16:1-3, 13).

Be sure to take advantage of the maps supplied with the course. Also remember to pray for wisdom each day before doing your work.

Unlike Joshua and Judges, most of the chapters in First Samuel are not associated with a Reference Point. Therefore, the course contains an overview of a majority of these chapters (without questions). You can cover such chapters by studying the overview only, or you can read the chapters in your Bible and follow by scanning the overview; whatever your time permits. Needless to say, it will be more beneficial to read both the chapters and the overview, but do what your time permits and nothing more. You don't want to get bogged down, for after all, you can study such chapters in more depth later.

1 Samuel 1 Elkanah, from the hill country of Ephraim, had wives named Peninnah and Hannah (vv.1-2). Peninnah bore children, but Hannah was barren (v.2). They went up yearly to worship at Shiloh where Eli and his two sons, Hophni and Phinehas, served as priests (v.3). Life was not pleasant for Hannah due to her barrenness (vv.1-8). After vowing that a son from her womb would be dedicated to the Lord (vv.9-11), Eli encouraged Hannah by saying, "Go in peace; and may the God of Israel grant your petition that you have asked of Him" (vv.12-17). Hannah was no longer saddened by her barrenness (v.18).

Elkanah and his family departed from Shiloh and returned to Ramah (v.19). Hannah then conceived and bore Samuel (v.20). Note: The exact location of Samuel's hometown, Ramah, is uncertain. It is positioned in Benjamin on the map titled *The Circuit of Samuel*, but this location may be incorrect.

Old Testament History　　　　　　　　*1 Samuel 1-19*　　　　　　　　*Week Five*

Elkanah made his annual trip to Shiloh (vv.21-22), but Hannah and Samuel remained in Ramah because Samuel was not yet weaned (vv.22-23). After he was weaned, Hannah took him to Shiloh to remain with Eli (vv.24-28). Leaving him must have been very difficult for her, but God rewarded Hannah's obedience.

Remember the names Ramah and Shiloh. Shiloh is where the tabernacle had rested since Joshua 18:1. Ramah was Samuel's hometown and an area he frequently visited while judging Israel.

<u>*1 Samuel 2*</u> Verses 1-10 record Hannah's prayer of praise which illustrates that most believers who suffer pain learn the importance of praise. After entrusting Samuel to Eli's care (and to God's sovereignty), Elkanah and Hannah returned to Ramah (v.11).

Eli's sons did not know the Lord, so they abused the sacrifices at Shiloh, taking what they wanted for personal use in a way contrary to Scripture (vv.12-17).

Hannah and Elkanah visited Samuel on a yearly basis, and Eli blessed them (vv.18-20). God honored them by allowing Hannah to bear three boys (in addition to Samuel) and two girls (v.21). These children confirm once again that you cannot give God more than He gives back in return. In the meantime, "Samuel grew before the Lord" (v.21).

Eli's two sons, Hophni and Phinehas, continued their ungodly lifestyle—even to the point of committing sexual acts with the women serving at the doorway of the tabernacle (vv.22-25). Samuel, however, "was growing in stature and in favor both with the Lord and with men" (v.26). A man of God revealed to Eli the consequences of his son's sin (vv.27-36). Many of Eli's descendants would be cut off from serving as priests at an early age (vv.31-32), a prophecy that is partially fulfilled when, for instance, only Abiathar escapes the massacre of the inhabitants of Nob (1 Samuel 22:18-20). However, King Solomon later dismisses Abiathar from the priesthood (1Kings 2:27). (Abiathar was the last priest to serve from the line of Ithamar, Eleazar's descendants served as high priests subsequent to his removal.) A sign would reveal the certainty of the prophecy described in 1Samuel 2:27-33—Hophni and Phinehas would die on the same day (v.34), and God would raise up a faithful high priest (vv.35-36), either pointing to Zadok, who served after Abiathar (1Kings 2:27, 35), or Christ. We will study these events in more detail as we work through the course. So, if you are confused at this juncture, know that you have plenty of time to sort it out.

<u>*1 Samuel 3*</u> "And word from the Lord was rare in those days, visions were infrequent" (v.1) due to the sin in Israel. However, God revealed to Samuel that all He had spoken against Eli because he had failed to rebuke his sons for their sin (v.13) would come to pass (vv.2-14). After Eli insisted, Samuel told him all that God had spoken (vv.15-18). Eli responded by saying, "It is the Lord; let Him do what seems good to Him" (v.18). As Samuel grew, the Lord was with him and none of his words failed (v.19). "All Israel from Dan even to Beersheba knew that Samuel was confirmed as a prophet of the Lord" (v.20). Note: The phrase "from Dan even to Beersheba" (v.20) is used often in the Old Testament. Dan was the city farthest north in Israel while Beersheba was the city farthest south. Thus, this phrase refers to all of Israel, which means that all Israel came to Shiloh to seek Samuel's counsel. Shiloh is where the Lord revealed Himself to Samuel through His word (v.21).

Second Day

<u>*1 Samuel 4*</u> Israel went out to fight the against the Philistines and camped beside Ebenezer (v.1). The Philistines camped at Aphek (v.1). After suffering defeat (v.2), Israel decided that the ark of the covenant was the only thing needed to guarantee victory (v.3). They brought the ark from Shiloh, and Hophni and Phinehas came along as well (v.4). Israel trusted in the symbol of God's presence (the ark of the covenant) rather than God Himself, which brought humiliating defeat (vv.5-10). The Philistines took the ark, and Hophni and Phinehas died (v.11).

Old Testament History *1 Samuel 1-19* Week Five

Eli received news that his two sons had died and that the ark had been taken by the Philistines (vv.12-17). When Eli received news of the ark, not the news of the death of his two sons, he fell off his seat and died (v.18). He had judged Israel for forty years (v.18). After receiving news of these events (v.19), Phinehas' wife, who was pregnant, instantly gave birth and then died, but not before naming her son "Ichabod" (vv.20-22). Ichabod means "no glory," for the glory departed from Israel when the ark was taken (vv.21-22).

1 Samuel 5 Use the map titled *The Journey of the Ark* (in the Reference Section) to find the cities mentioned in this chapter. The Philistines first took the ark to Ashdod (v.1). However, when their god, Dagon, fell twice on his face before it—and even had his head cut off his shoulders as well as his two palms (vv.2-5)—and when God ravaged and smote the Ashdodites with tumors (v.6), they sent the ark away (vv.7-8). When the ark came to Gath (v.8), another Philistine city, God brought confusion and smote the men of the city with tumors (v.9). They then sent the ark to Ekron (v.10), where the same thing occurred that had occurred in Gath—more confusion and more tumors (vv.11-12). The Lord can take care of Himself. Why then do we attempt to fight His battles for Him instead of allowing Him to fight His battles through us (Galatians 2:20; Philippians 2:13)?

1 Samuel 6 After the ark had been in Philistine territory for seven months (v.1), the Philistines desired to send it home—back to Israel (v.2). They were fed up with all the turmoil it had caused. They called for the priests and diviners (v.2) who suggested that a guilt offering of five golden tumors and five golden mice be sent with the ark (vv.3-6). (Verse 6 indicates that these diviners and priests understood well God's ability to deliver His people. We can rest assured that our enemy, the deceiver of the brethren, understands the same today.) The ark, along with the guilt offerings, was sent on a cart drawn by two milch cows on which had never been a yoke (vv.7-8). (The phrase "milch cows" refers to cows with nursing calves. If you were raised on a farm, you know that it is next to impossible to separate a cow from her nursing calf, which makes these events even more interesting. Also, the guilt offerings offered by the Philistines had nothing to do with the removal of God's judgment. These offerings were not in compliance with God's Law and were therefore rejected. They only confirmed the Philistines' commitment to their own methods of worship rather than repentance and submission to God.) The fact that the cart traveled to Beth-shemesh (vv.10-15) confirmed that it was God who had brought judgment on the Philistines (v.9) and that Jehovah God is sovereign over all. Find Beth-shemesh on the map titled *The Journey of the Ark*.

The cart and cows were offered to God (v.14) because anything used for sacred purposes could not be used for the secular. Also, this offering at Beth-shemesh was proper because of the desolation of Shiloh. According to the Talmud and various Jewish authorities, sacrifices were permitted at various locations during this time because no central sanctuary existed in Israel. Thus, this offering was not in violation of Deuteronomy 12:10-14. Try to imagine what the five lords of the Philistines thought and felt as they looked on (v.16). The offerings they had sent with the ark are mentioned in verses 17-18.

The men at Beth-shemesh should have known better than to look into the ark, the dwelling place of Jehovah. God struck many of them (v.19), which caused the inhabitants of Beth-shemesh to encourage men from Kiriath-jearim to take the ark (vv.20-21).

1 Samuel 7:1-2 The men of Kiriath-jearim took the ark from Beth-shemesh (v.1), and it remained in Kiriath-jearim for twenty years (v.2). While it was there, Israel lamented after the Lord (v.2).

Third Day

Read 1 Samuel 7. Verses 3-17 are associated with Reference Point 41, *Samuel Rules as Last Judge of Israel*.

Old Testament History   *1 Samuel 1-19*   **Week Five**

1. According to 1 Samuel 7:3, what would bring victory over the Philistines? How did Israel respond to Samuel's suggestion? What did Samuel ask of Israel in verse 5? Find Mizpah (or Mizpeh) on the *General Map of Israel* in the Reference Section. What does verse 6 state about Samuel? Remember that Samuel replaced Eli as judge of Israel.

2. What did the Philistines do in response to Israel's gathering at Mizpah? How did Israel then respond (vv.7-8)? What was Samuel's response (v.9)? What resulted (vv.10-11)?

3. God routed the Philistines. What made the difference between this battle and their previous one when the Philistines captured the ark? What does this deciding factor tell you about the power of prayer? If you are not satisfied with your prayer life, what positive steps can you take for improvement?

4. What did Samuel do in verse 12? What does verse 13 tell us about the Philistines? About Samuel? God honors faithful leaders! What does verse 14 state about the land?

5. How long did Samuel judge Israel (v.15)? Where did he judge Israel (vv.16-17)? Use the map titled *The Circuit of Samuel* (in the Reference Section). Samuel spent much time traveling between these cities as he judged God's people. You are growing!

1 Samuel 8 When Samuel was old, he appointed his sons as judges (v.1), and they judged the people in Beersheba (v.2). They were ungodly men (v.3), so the elders asked that Samuel might appoint a king to judge them "like all the nations" (vv.4-5). Their request displeased Samuel (v.6), but God revealed that the people were rejecting Him instead of Samuel (vv.7-8). Samuel was to warn the people concerning what a king would demand (v.9-18). How Israel could desire a king after hearing all the negatives recorded in verses 10-18 is baffling. Sin blinds those who walk in disobedience. The peoples' minds were set. They desired a king so they could "be like all the nations" and have him fight their battles (vv.19-20). God then consented to their wishes (vv.21-22). We will now see what Israel reaps from rejecting God as her King.

1 Samuel 9 Saul, of the tribe of Benjamin, was the tallest and one of the most handsome men in Israel (vv.1-2). (These attributes in no way qualify a person for leadership.) When Kish, his father,

Old Testament History *1 Samuel 1-19* *Week Five*

lost his donkeys, Saul and a servant went to find them (v.3). After searching for some time (vv.4-5), the servant suggested that they seek Samuel for help (vv.6-9)—Samuel is referred to as "a man of God" (vv.6, 7, 8, and 10). Saul agreed (v.10), but the fact that he knew nothing of Samuel (vv.6-7) confirms his lack of interest in the things of God, especially since they lived in the same tribal territory (Benjamin). The city where Saul and the servant sought Samuel was probably Ramah.

After receiving information as to Samuel's whereabouts (vv.11-13), they entered the city and Samuel came toward them (v.14). (From what is stated in verse 13, Saul should have learned that it was Samuel's responsibility alone to bless the sacrifice.) God had revealed to Samuel the previous day that Saul would come to him (v.15-16). He also revealed that Saul would be king and deliver Israel from the Philistines (vv.15-16). When Samuel saw Saul, God spoke to Samuel and confirmed that Saul would rule over Israel (v.17). Samuel told Saul that the donkeys had been found and that he would lead Israel (vv.18-20). Due to Saul's insecurity, which will surface many times over the next several chapters, Saul stated that he was from the smallest tribe in Israel (Benjamin) as well as the least significant family within that tribe (v.21). Verse 1, however, confirms just the opposite. Saul's father was "a mighty man of valor"—a man of wealth and influence. But Saul, because of a lack of character, shunned responsibility throughout his lifetime. Therefore, he balked at the idea of leading God's people. However, he was right in saying that Benjamin was the smallest tribe in Israel (v.21), which resulted from the events of Judges 19-21.

Saul and the servant had dinner on the high place with Samuel (along with about thirty other men—vv.22-24) and departed the next morning (vv.25-26). As they were leaving the city, Samuel asked that the servant might go ahead of them so he could proclaim God's word to Saul (v.27).

Fourth Day

Read 1 Samuel 10, which is associated with Reference Point 42, *Saul Becomes First King of Israel*.

1. What did Samuel do to Saul in verse 1? What did these actions confirm (v.1)? Some of the supernatural events that verified Saul's position of leadership are described in verses 2-7 and 9-13. Which one of these intrigues you the most? Why? What did Samuel instruct Saul to do at Gilgal (v.8)?

2. In your opinion, why would Saul refrain from telling his uncle the whole truth about these developments (vv.14-16)?

3. What impressed you the most about the ceremony recorded in verses 17-25? What disheartened you about it? What does the first sentence in verse 19 communicate to you? Who went with Saul to his home in Gibeah?

Old Testament History   *1 Samuel 1-19*   **Week Five**

1 Samuel 11 Saul (of Gibeah) has instant success by defeating the Ammonites who came against Jabesh-gilead (vv.1-13). (The Ammonites were descendants of Lot, Genesis 19:36-38.) Saul numbered his troops at Bezek (v.8) before entering the battle. After defeating the Ammonites, Samuel suggested they go to Gilgal and "renew the kingdom" (v.14). Samuel's instructions were followed "and there they made Saul king before the Lord in Gilgal" (v.15). They also offered sacrifices to the Lord and rejoiced (v.15). However, Saul's initial success was short lived. A man's leadership abilities (as well as his character) are proven over the long haul—not the short term!

1 Samuel 12 In an address to the nation, Samuel reviews his faithfulness to Israel (vv.1-5) He also reviews God's faithfulness to the nation (vv.6-11). He then reminds them of the wickedness they had displayed by asking for a king (vv.12-17). He even called for rain and thunder to confirm God's displeasure with their decision (v.18). The people repented for desiring a king (v.19), and Samuel assured them of God's continued devotion to the nation (vv.20-24). However, if they disobeyed both they and their king would "be swept away" (v.25).

1 Samuel 13 The exact length of Saul's reign and the age in which he began to reign (v.1) are hard to determine because most of the numbers that could give us such information have not survived with the original Hebrew text. (The numbers "forty" and "thirty" are in italics, which means they have been inserted.)

After Jonathan, Saul's son, smote the garrison of the Philistines at Geba (vv.2-3), the people were summoned to Saul at Gilgal (v.4). The Philistines then assembled an army of 30,000 chariots and 6,000 horsemen and camped at Michmash (v.5)—near Geba (Michmash is about three miles from Ramah and on the direct route from Ramah to Gilgal). When the men of Israel understood the magnitude of what they were facing, they were frightened (vv.6-7), and the people with Saul trembled (v.7)—the natural response when your leader is incapable of viewing life from God's perspective. The Philistines were no problem for God, but rather a tool for training Israel to fight spiritual battles with spiritual weapons.

When Samuel delayed in coming to Gilgal, and when the people began to scatter, Saul disobeyed Samuel's command of 1 Samuel 10:8 and offered the burnt offering (vv.8-9). As soon as Saul did so Samuel arrived (v.10). (Evidently this offering was for the purpose of bringing God's favor upon the people—vv.11-12.) This act of disobedience (which revealed a much deeper problem in Saul—that of flawed character) cost Saul his kingdom. None of his sons would rule in Israel after his death (vv.13-14).

Samuel departed (v.15), and Saul and the Philistines prepared for battle (vv.15-23). Saul's army, however, had neither sword nor spear due to previous Philistine oppression (vv.19-22). Therefore, God had Israel exactly where He wanted them. Only through His supernatural power could Israel prevail.

Fifth Day

1 Samuel 14 Jonathan, Saul's son, a godly man, along with his armor bearer, approached the Philistine camp and slew about twenty men (vv.1-14). This massacre caused trembling in the Philistine camp (v.15). (Jonathan had told no one where he and his armor bearer were going.) When Saul's watchmen observed that the Philistines were melting away (v.16), Israel pursued and overpowered them (vv.16-23). However, Saul spoiled the victory by placing everyone under an oath, saying, "Cursed be the man who eats food before evening, and until I have avenged myself on my enemies" (v.24). This mistake was huge. Since Jonathan was unaware of the oath, he ate honey and was strengthened (vv.25-27). When Saul attempted to put Jonathan to death (for breaking the oath—vv.28-44), the people would not allow it (v.45). Saul stopped pursuing the Philistines after this incident, and the Philistines "went to their own place" (v.46).

Old Testament History *1 Samuel 1-19* Week Five

Even though Saul experienced great success as a warrior (vv.47-48) and had an outstanding captain in Abner (v.50) and attached mighty and valiant men to his staff (v.52), his lack of character served as his Achilles' heel.

The important aspect of this chapter is that Jonathan served as the catalyst that brought courage to the hearts of Israel. God's people were gripped with fear because of the brute strength of their enemy. However, when Jonathan did his part (in destroying the portion of the enemy that God had assigned him), Israel entered battle with what remained. These events illustrate that as we individually trust God to cast out the enemy in our homes, workplaces, and everywhere, others will desire to do the same.

1 Samuel 15 Because of what Amalek did to Israel while coming out of Egypt (vv.1-2; Exodus 17:8-16; Deuteronomy 25:17-19), Saul was to destroy all the Amalekites—no spoils were to be taken and nothing was to remain alive (v.3). Saul defeated the Amalekites but spared king Agag and the best of the spoils (vv.4-9). Samuel approached Saul and questioned why he had disobeyed (vv.10-14). Saul blamed the people (v.15), but Samuel rebuked him for his disobedience (vv.16-19). Then Saul stated that the people took the spoils to have something to sacrifice to God (vv.20-21). Samuel responded that obedience is better than sacrifice (v.22). Samuel then told Saul that God had rejected him as king (v.23). After Saul somewhat repented (v.24-25), and after Samuel assured him that his kingdom had been given to someone else (vv.26-29), Samuel returned with him to the people (vv.30-31). Samuel then hewed king Agag to pieces at Gilgal (vv.32-33). Samuel went to Ramah (his hometown) and Saul went to his home in Gibeah (v.34). Samuel never saw Saul again (v.35).

This chapter teaches that we should not blame our disobedience on someone else and that God prefers obedience over sacrifice. Saul's lack of character brought his downfall.

1 Samuel 16 God sent Samuel to Bethlehem to anoint David as king (vv.1-13), and "the Spirit of the Lord came mightily upon David from that day forward" (v.13). Samuel then left for Ramah (v.13). God looks at the heart of a man instead of his appearance (v.7)—all of David's brothers "looked" more qualified for the job than he.

On those occasions when an evil spirit terrorized Saul, David played his harp and the spirit would depart (vv.14-23). Saul did not realize that David had been anointed king, or he would not have allowed David to join his staff.

When God says, "Now the Spirit of the Lord departed from Saul" (v.14), He does not mean that Saul lost his salvation, but rather that he lost the anointing that he had as King of Israel. Second, the evil spirit that terrorized him (v.14) was not sent from God's person (for God is totally perfect and holy), but rather was used by God to accomplish His purpose.

Sixth Day

1 Samuel 17 This chapter is very familiar, for here David slays Goliath. The chapter begins with Saul and Israel preparing to fight the Philistines (vv.1-3). When Goliath of Gath, a Philistine giant, demanded that Israel send a man against him (vv.4-10), all of Israel was "dismayed and greatly afraid" (v.11). However, David, after arriving at Israel's camp (vv.12-30), went against the Philistine giant and killed him (vv.31-51). David chose to fight Goliath because he desired "that all the earth may know that there is a God in Israel, and that all this assembly may know that the Lord does not deliver by sword or by spear; for the battle is the Lord's" (vv.46-47). Wow!
David's goal was to live life for what God got out of it rather than for what he got out of it, which is why God could place David in charge of His kingdom. After David's act of valor, Israel slew many Philistines and plundered the Philistine camps (vv.52-53). David then took Goliath's head

Old Testament History   *1 Samuel 1-19*   **Week Five**

to Jerusalem, but he put Goliath's weapons in his tent (v.54). Verses 55-58 record the information that David gave Abner and Saul concerning his family background.

The most important of the lessons to learn from this chapter is that God can do the impossible if we will but view life from His perspective. To David, Goliath was nothing more than an uncircumcised Philistine (v.26)—the exact way God viewed him. However, to Saul and Israel he was an overwhelming enemy impossible to destroy. Since God's perspective is gained through a proper understanding of His word, aren't you excited about the benefits associated with what you are learning?

1 Samuel 18 As soon as David had finished speaking with Saul, Jonathan's soul was knit to David's soul and "Jonathan loved him as himself" (v.1). Jonathan and David would get more time together since Saul prohibited David from returning to his father (v.2). Jonathan even made a covenant with David by stripping himself of his robe and armor, including his sword, bow, and belt (vv.3-4). This covenant made David and Jonathan responsible to one another for life. It also symbolized that everything belonging to Jonathan now belonged to David, and vice versa. They were co-owners of what each possessed, and if either should die, the surviving party was responsible for caring for the deceased party's offspring. This covenant will play a major role in David's response to Jonathan's offspring once David takes the throne. (We entered into a covenant with Jesus Christ the moment we accepted Him as Savior—1 Corinthians 11:25. All He owns belongs to us, and all we own belongs to Him. He will also be faithful to us forever. Wow!)

Wherever Saul sent David, David prospered (v.5). In fact, it pleased all of Israel when Saul set him over the men of war, including Saul's servants (v.5). But when David returned from killing Goliath, the women of Israel sang, "Saul has slain his thousands, and David his ten thousands" (vv.6-7), which bred jealousy on Saul's part, and his and David's relationship was never the same (vv.8-9). The next day Saul tried to spear David, but David escaped on two different occasions (vv.10-11).

The reason Saul feared David was because God's spirit had departed from him and now rested on David (v.12). As far as Saul was concerned, the most logical thing to do was place David in as dangerous an environment as possible—in battle against Israel's foes (v.13). But everywhere David turned God caused him to prosper (vv.14-16).

To try to hurt David, Saul promised David his daughter (Merab) but gave her instead to another man (vv.17-19). He then promised David his other daughter, Michal, in exchange for one hundred foreskins of the Philistines (vv.20-25). Saul considered this task impossible, and assumed David would die trying to fulfill this obligation (v.25). Instead, David brought Saul two hundred Philistine foreskins (twice as many as had been requested), David received Michal as his wife, and Saul feared David even more (vv.26-29). David was wiser in battle than any of Saul's servants, and "his name was highly esteemed" (v.30).

This chapter teaches: (1) jealousy destroys relationships (as well as those it possesses); (2) God's supernatural protection rests on those who walk in humble submission.

1 Samuel 19 Saul's passion to destroy David continues. Saul told Jonathan, as well as his servants, to put David to death (v.1), but Jonathan convinced him to restore David to a place of favor (vv.2-7). But after David experienced more success against the Philistines, Saul again displayed his hostility by trying to kill him (vv.8-10). Saul even tried to seize David at his home, but Michal (Saul's daughter and David's wife) deceived Saul's men and David escaped (vv.11-17). David fled to Samuel at Ramah, they then traveled to Naioth, and when Saul's men came to seize David, the Spirit of God came upon these men (on three separate occasions) and they prophesied (vv.18-21). Saul prophesied as well when he came to apprehend David (vv.22-24). (Saul had also prophesied in 1 Samuel 10:10-11, but we can't assume in either case that he was functioning as a true prophet functioned in his day.) Thus, the Spirit of God supernaturally protected David, for he fled from

Old Testament History   ***1 Samuel 1-19***   ***Week Five***

Ramah in 1 Samuel 20:1.

No one can read this chapter without coming to a deeper appreciation of God's sovereignty and absolute control of things. God protects His people in the most unique ways. David could have sat for years and never imagined that God would deliver him in such a unique manner. God could do the same for you this very day!

Old Testament History   *1 Samuel 20—2 Samuel 6*   *Week Six*

The History Books of the Old Testament

Week Six

First Day

This week you will study 1 Samuel 20 through 2 Samuel 6. The course contains an overview of most of these chapters (without questions). As was stated earlier in the course, you can cover such chapters by studying the overview only, or you can read the chapters in your Bible and follow by scanning the overview. Follow the path your time permits. Don't forget to pray for wisdom!

1 Samuel 20 David departed from Ramah and approached Jonathan (v.1) for the purpose of finding out if Saul's hostility toward him had subsided. Jonathan, his covenant partner, was the perfect man to seek out such information. Jonathan agreed to do so (vv.2-9), and a plan was devised to communicate Jonathan's findings to David (vv.10-23). In the process they also renewed their covenant (vv.14-17). (Jonathan realized that the kingdom would go to David and not himself. Therefore, he wanted assurance that David would care for his family.) When Jonathan questioned Saul concerning his feelings about David, Saul attempted to kill Jonathan, so he departed to find David (vv.24-34). Jonathan warned David (vv.35-40), and with much sorrow these covenant brothers went their separate ways (vv.41-42).

This chapter reveals the strength of the covenant that David and Jonathan sealed in 1 Samuel 18:3-4. They loved one another, and were faithful to one another, to death. Since through faith and repentance we enter a covenant with Jesus, we should be faithful to one another as well.

1 Samuel 21 David fled to Nob and approached Ahimelech the high priest (v.1), deceiving him into believing that he was about the king's business (v.2). (Ahimelech was a descendant of Eli—1 Samuel 22:11; 14:3.) David and his men ate the consecrated bread from the holy place of the house of God (vv.2-6; Leviticus 24:5-9; Matthew 12:4). However, Doeg the Edomite, "the chief of Saul's shepherds," observed what had occurred (v.7), which brings major repercussions in the next chapter. (Doeg may have joined Saul after Saul attacked Edom in 1 Samuel 14:47.) David also took the sword of Goliath (the Philistine), which had been wrapped in a cloth and kept behind the ephod (vv.8-9). (An ephod was a sleeveless linen vest worn by the priests. The high priest had a brightly colored ephod with twelve gemstones attached to the chest piece.) No other sword was like this one (v.9) in that it reminded David of God's faithfulness. David fled to Gath (v.10—in Philistine territory), evidently thinking Achish, king of Gath, was aware of his and Saul's conflict. But the Philistines were unnerved by David's presence (since he was a Jew and a great warrior), so David pretended to be insane and thus viewed as less threatening (vv.10-15). Again, David used deception for his own personal gain.

In this chapter David used deception for two purposes: (1) To have his physical needs met; (2) As a means of protection. The next chapter confirms that his sin carried a high price. Had David chosen not to flee, all would have been well. God had selected him to rule (1 Samuel 16:1). Therefore, nothing could take his life until He did. However, his irresponsible behavior brought severe consequences.

1 Samuel 22 David departed from Gath to reside at the cave of Adullam (v.1). His family followed him, including his brothers and his father's household (v.1). This safety precaution was employed since entire families were, in some cases, put to death for the fault of one of its members, which will be confirmed shortly with Ahimelech. Many misfits came to David as well (v.2). David's love for God and God's people caused men from a variety of backgrounds to honor and respect him. David then found refuge in Moab for his father and mother (vv.3-4), which may have been

43

Old Testament History   *1 Samuel 20—2 Samuel 6*   *Week Six*

possible because Ruth, a Moabite, was David's great-grandmother (Ruth 4:13-22). The prophet Gad (mentioned for the first time in Scripture) instructed David to leave his present stronghold and move to the land of Judah (v.5).

After Saul complained about his servant's lack of loyalty (vv.6-8), Doeg the Edomite revealed that Ahimelech had assisted David (vv.9-10). Saul then had Doeg kill Ahimelech and Ahimelech's father's household (vv.11-18), which included the priests of Nob (eighty-five men). Doeg also struck the remaining inhabitants of Nob—along with the animals (v.19). Abiathar, son of Ahimelech, was the only one to escape (v.20). Abiathar fled to David and reported what had occurred (vv.20-21). Then, David realized his deceit had brought death to every person in Abiathar's father's household (v.22). Wow! David encouraged Abiathar to remain with him (v.23). (What happened to Abiathar's family was a fulfillment of what the man of God had told Eli in 1 Samuel 2:31. Review your notes on 1 Samuel 2:27-36)

Second Day

1 Samuel 23 David and his men delivered the inhabitants of Keilah from the Philistines (vv.1-5), but only after seeking God's will in the matter (vv.2 and 4). When Saul received word that David was in Keilah, he prepared to attack him (vv.7-8). When David heard of Saul's plan, he asked for the ephod (v.9) that had been brought to him by Abiathar (v.6). He then sought God's guidance by asking if the inhabitants of Keilah would surrender him to Saul (vv.10-12). God confirmed that they would, and David departed (vv.12-13), at which time Saul temporarily ceased to pursue him (v.13).

After leaving Keilah, David and his men camped in the wilderness of Ziph, and Saul sought every day (to no avail) to destroy him (v.14). At Horesh, Jonathan came to David "and encouraged him in God" (vv.15-16). He reminded David that Saul would not find him and that David would be king (v.17). Even though Jonathan anticipated being next to David in David's kingdom (v.17), Jonathan will die in battle before David takes the throne. After Jonathan and David made a covenant before the Lord, Jonathan returned to his house while David remained in Horesh (v.18).

The Ziphites betrayed David by telling Saul of David's whereabouts (vv.19-20). However, by the time Saul arrived David had moved to the wilderness of Maon (vv.21-25). At the point that Saul was about to surround David, Saul received news that the Philistines had "made a raid on the land" (vv.26-27). Saul ceased pursuing David and returned to fight the Philistines (v.28). Again, the sovereignty of God protected His anointed. David then went to stay in "the strongholds of Engedi" (v.29).

Can you believe how God honored David's humility and willingness to submit to authority? Isn't it amazing that David has not once tried to strike back at Saul? This story ties in well with Romans 12:17-21.

1 Samuel 24 After Saul finished with the Philistines, he pursued David at Engedi (vv.1-2). When Saul entered a cave to relieve himself (a cave where David and his men were hiding), instead of killing Saul (even after David's men tried to convince him to do so), David secretly cut off the edge of Saul's robe (vv.3-4). After doing so, David's conscience pricked him, and he refused to allow his men to take Saul's life (vv.5-7). David departed out of the cave and called to Saul (v.8). Saul turned, and David bowed and prostrated himself (v.8). While holding the edge of Saul's robe, David tried to explain that he held no animosity toward him (vv.9-15). Saul wept and spoke kindly of David—even to the point of asking that David care for his offspring once he reigned as king (vv.16-21). David agreed to do so, Saul departed and went home, "but David and his men went up to the stronghold" (v.22).

What encourages me here is that David was not easily swayed by peer pressure, and that he had a

Old Testament History 1 Samuel 20—2 Samuel 6 Week Six

sensitivity to wrong—regardless of how slight the wrong (vv.4-7). May we possess the character needed to respond similarly during adversity.

1 Samuel 25 Samuel died and was buried in Ramah (his hometown), and David went to the wilderness of Paran (v.1). Because Samuel was the spiritual leader of Israel until his death, his departure meant that Israel would be without spiritual guidance until the reign of David.

Most of this chapter deals with a man named Nabal (of Maon), his wife Abigail, and David. (You can find Maon on the *General Map of Israel* included in the reference section.) David had been protecting Nabal's work force, so David requested compensation (vv.2-9). Nabal refused (vv.10-11), and as David was preparing to retaliate (vv.12-13), one of Nabal's workmen informed Abigail of David's protection and persistent goodwill (vv.14-16). He also informed her of the impending disaster awaiting Nabal's household (v.17). Abigail quickly took food and wine to David—even pronounced a blessing on Israel's future king (vv.18-31). David then dismissed Abigail in peace (vv.32-35). Soon after Abigail told Nabal of these events, he died (vv.36-38). David then married Abigail (vv.39-42), even though he had also taken Ahinoam of Jezreel to be his wife (v.43). Saul had given David's first wife, Michal, Saul's daughter, to Palti from Gallim (v.44).

The Lord is preparing David for his future rulership over Israel. Adversity is a wonderful tool to teach men to lead.

Third Day

1 Samuel 26 The Ziphites again betrayed David by telling Saul of his whereabouts (v.1). Saul came to the wilderness of Ziph, where David camped (vv.2-3). While Saul slept, David and Abishai slipped into Saul's camp and stole his spear and jug of water (vv.4-12). While there, Abishai desired to take Saul's life, but David refused to let him strike "the Lord's anointed" (vv.8-9). David would trust God to take Saul's life when He so desired (v.10). What character David possessed!

David and Abishai departed, but David called to Saul's camp from a distance (vv.13-14). David accused Abner, Saul's captain (1 Samuel 14:50), of failing to protect the king (vv.15-16). After all, Abishai would have taken Saul's life had David not intervened. When Saul recognized David's voice (v.17), David spoke of his innocence and pleaded that Saul refrain from pursuing him (vv.18-20). David's words brought sorrow (not repentance) to Saul's heart (v.21), and after reminding Saul that he spared his life (vv.22-24), Saul blessed David (v.25).

It is hard to believe that a man of David's character could later commit adultery and murder. What a powerful statement this should make to all the redeemed.

1 Samuel 27 Due to David's fear of Saul, which resulted from a lack of faith, David moved to Philistine territory (v.1). Remember that God had Samuel anoint David as the next king of Israel in 1 Samuel 16:1-13. Therefore, nothing could take his life, not even Saul. David and his family, along with his men and their families, lived with Achish, the Philistine king of Gath (vv.2-3). (Look at the map *The Journey of the Ark* to see the location of Gath.) When Saul received news of David's whereabouts, he ceased pursuing David (v.4).

Achish gave Ziklag to David as a place for him and his men to reside (vv.5-6). David lived in Philistine territory for a year and four months (v.7), until Saul's death. While there he carried out raids against the Geshurites, the Girzites, and the Amalekites (v.8)—nomadic tribes that were a nuisance both to the Philistines and Israel. David left no one alive when he made such raids (v.9) so he could deceive Achish into believing he had fought against Israel (vv.10-11). Thus, Achish considered David to be "odious among his people Israel" and his servant forever (v.12).

Old Testament History *1 Samuel 20—2 Samuel 6* *Week Six*

1 Samuel 28 The Philistines gathered to fight against Israel, and Achish asked David to join them (v.1) and he agreed (v.2). King Saul, on the other hand, was in a real fix. Samuel was dead, which meant that he had no one to turn to for godly counsel (v.3). Saul had even removed the ungodly mediums and spiritists (Leviticus 19:31; 20:27; Deuteronomy 18:10-11) from Israel (v.3). When the Philistines gathered against Israel at Shunem, Saul gathered his troops at Gilboa (v.4). However, Saul became frightened when he perceived the size of the Philistine army (v.5), which caused him to inquire of the Lord, but the Lord did not answer (v.6). Saul then turned to a medium in Endor (vv.7-8), and after guaranteeing that no punishment would befall her (for being a medium), she brought Samuel up from the dead (vv.9-14). (Whether or not this was Samuel is still up for debate. But Saul believed it was Samuel. If Samuel truly appeared, he came not as a result of the woman's witchcraft, but rather by God's supernatural powers.) Saul learned of his fate through this being; he, his sons, and Israel would fall at the hands of the Philistines (vv.15-19). This news devastated Saul, but after eating, he and his men departed (vv.20-25).

Saul's life illustrates that sin and disobedience result in an inability to hear from God (vv.6 and 15). We must never forget this truth! This chapter also validates the importance of surrounding ourselves with those who can provide wise, godly counsel.

Fourth Day

1 Samuel 29 The Philistines gathered at Aphek, while Israel camped by the spring in Jezreel (v.1). David and his men proceeded with the Philistines (v.2), but the Philistine commanders were concerned by his presence (vv.3-5). Finally, king Achish, at the insistence of the Philistine commanders, advised them to return to their home in Ziklag (vv.6-11). The Philistines then proceeded to Jezreel to war with Israel (v.11).

1 Samuel 30 When David and his men returned home, they found that the Amalekites had burned Ziklag to the ground (v.1). They had also taken the women and children (everyone who was in the city) but had not killed any of them (vv.2-3). When David and his men saw what had occurred, they "lifted their voices and wept until there was no strength in them to weep" (v.4). Even Ahinoam and Abigail (David's two wives) had been taken (v.5). David not only had this problem with which to deal, but his men, the men to whom he had given his life, also spoke of stoning him (v.6). And how do you suppose he coped? Simple! "David strengthened himself in the Lord his God" (v.6). Psalm 27:1-6, penned by David, explains why this man of God could find peace in the midst of such turmoil.

When David inquired of the Lord, he was told to pursue the Amalekites and take back all that was lost (vv.7-8). David did so, defeating the Amalekites and recovering the spoils (vv.9-25). He later sent some of these spoils to Judah "and to all the places where David himself and his men were accustomed to go" (vv.26-31).

The highlight of this chapter is David's godly response to adversity along with God's faithful response to David.

1 Samuel 31 The Philistines killed Saul's men on Mount Gilboa (v.1), along with Jonathan, Abinadab, and Malchi-shua, three of Saul's sons (v.2). When Saul was badly wounded by Philistine archers, he asked that his armor bearer kill him before the Philistines arrived (vv.3-4). When his armor bearer refused, Saul fell on his own sword (v.4), and his armor bearer took his own life (v.5). Thus, Saul and his men died on Mount Gilboa (v.6).

When the men of Israel fled, the Philistines lived in their abandoned cities (v.7). The Philistines even cut off Saul's head and sent it, along with his weapons, throughout Philistine territory (vv.8-9). They eventually "put his weapons in the temple of Ashtaroth" and "fastened his body to the

Old Testament History *1 Samuel 20—2 Samuel 6* *Week Six*

wall of Beth-shan" (v.10). Valiant men from Jabesh-gilead took Saul's body, along with his son's bodies, off the wall of Beth-shan, brought them to Jabesh, burned them, and buried them (vv.11-13). If you wonder why men from Jabesh-gilead had such compassion for Saul, review your notes on 1 Samuel 11.

The stage is now set. Saul is dead, along with David's faithful friend, Jonathan. In 2 Samuel we will observe how David and Jonathan's covenant affected David's decisions as king.

Fifth Day

Welcome to 2 Samuel. First and 2 Samuel were originally one book, but with the development of the Septuagint (a translation of the Old Testament from Hebrew to Greek) the book was divided.

The first four chapters of 2 Samuel are located between Reference Points 42 and 43. Don't forget to ask for wisdom as you study these chapters (James 1:5).

2 Samuel 1 After David returned from slaughtering the Amalekites, and while he was still at Ziklag (v.1), an Amalekite came to him (vv.2-3). He reported that many in Israel had fallen, that Jonathan was dead, and that he had taken Saul's life upon Saul's request (vv.4-10). He even brought Saul's crown and bracelet to validate his words (v.10).

How Saul actually died differed from the Amalekite's account (compare 1 Samuel 31:1-6), but thinking that David would be elated over Saul's death (and honor him for killing the king), he lied to make himself the "hero." However, David mourned, wept, and fasted when he heard the news of Saul, Jonathan, and the men of Israel (vv.11-12). He even had the Amalekite put to death (vv.13-16) for saying he had "killed the Lord's anointed" (v.16). (I believe David realized the Amalekite hadn't killed Saul, but was lying for personal gain.) The Amalekite died for something he did not do. Deceit never pays, especially when used for the purpose of self-exaltation!

Verses 17-27 confirm David's love for Saul and Jonathan. Normally, professional mourners, usually women (Jeremiah 9:17) lamented for the dead (2 Chronicles 35:25). Not so here. David did it himself (v.17) and charged the people to learn the lament as well (v.18). This lament was also recorded in the book of Jashar. (The book of Jashar—v.17; Joshua 10:13—contained the history of the wars of God's people.)

2 Samuel 2 After David sought God's guidance concerning a move to Judah, God instructed David to go to Hebron, in Judah (v.1). David moved, along with his family, his men, and their families (vv.2-3). Upon David's arrival, the men of Judah anointed him king over Judah (v.4). After learning that the men of Jabesh-gilead buried Saul's body (Jabesh-gilead is east of the Jordan), David commended them (vv.4-7), which may have been done for political reasons. Abner, who had served as Saul's commander, had taken Ish-bosheth, Saul's son, and made him king over Israel (vv.8-9). He had done so at Mahanaim—which was east of the Jordan (vv.8-9).

During Ish-bosheth's two-year reign over the house of Israel, the house of Judah followed David (v.10). (David reigned over Judah from Hebron seven years and six months—v.11.) Abner and Ish-bosheth's servants were defeated by Joab and David's servants at Gibeon (vv.12-17). But Asahel, Joab's brother (v.18), was killed while pursuing Abner (vv.19-23). Joab and Abishai (Joab's other brother—v.18) pursued Abner until he convinced them to stop fighting against their fellow Hebrews (vv.24-28). Abner and his men returned to Mahanaim (v.29), and Joab and his men, after burying Asahel in Bethlehem, returned to Hebron (vv.30-32).

Old Testament History *1 Samuel 20—2 Samuel 6* *Week Six*

The kingdom was divided at this time—*Israel* under Ish-bosheth and *Judah* under David. Remember the names Abner and Joab.

2 Samuel 3 As the war continued between the house of Saul and the house of David, the house of Saul grew weaker and weaker (v.1). David had six sons while at Hebron, all by different wives (vv.2-5). Meanwhile, Abner became a powerful force in the house of Saul (v.6). In fact, when Ish-bosheth accused him of going in to Saul's concubine (vv.7-8), Abner sought to attach himself and all of Israel to David (vv.9-12). But Abner could meet with David only if he brought Michal, Saul's daughter and David's first wife (v.13). After David sent messengers to Ish-bosheth, Michal was taken from her husband, Paltiel (vv.14-16), the man to whom Saul had given her in 1 Samuel 25:44.

After Abner and all Israel agreed to make David their king, Abner approached David with the proposition and David accepted (vv.17-21). At this time Michal was returned to David. Abner then departed to gather Israel to David (v.21). When Joab discovered what had occurred (vv.22-23), he reprimanded David for allowing Abner in his presence (vv.24-25), secretly sent messengers to apprehend Abner (v.26), and he and Abishai avenged the blood of their brother Asahel by killing Abner in Hebron (vv.27 and 30). When the men of Israel observed David's response to Abner's death, along with his harsh words toward Joab (vv.28-29, 31-35), they understood that David was innocent in the matter (vv.36-37). The chapter ends with David praising Abner and expressing even more harsh words toward Joab and Abishai (vv.38-39).

Sixth Day

2 Samuel 4 Ish-bosheth lost courage (in fact all Israel was disturbed) when they heard of Abner's death in Hebron (vv.1-3). Jonathan's son, Mephibosheth, a very important individual (as we see later), is mentioned in verse 4. He was lame due to falling while fleeing after Saul and Jonathan's death (v.4). Rechab and Baanah, commanders of Ish-bosheth's bands (v.2), killed Ish-bosheth and beheaded him (vv.5-7). Upon bringing his head to David, David had them killed (vv.8-12). He even had Ish-bosheth's head buried in Abner's grave (v.12). David was enraged with Rechab and Baanah's actions.

Twice David has responded righteously after hearing of an enemy's death (both with Saul and Ish-bosheth). How does that relate to why God considered David a man after His own heart (1 Samuel 13:14)? How can we adopt a similar attitude toward our enemies?

Read 2 Samuel 5:1-5, which is associated with Reference Point 43, *David Becomes Second King of Israel,* is associated with these verses.

1. Where was David when he was anointed king over Israel? How long did David reign over Judah, and from where did he reign? How long did he reign over Judah and Israel, and from where did he reign?

David did not become king of both Israel and Judah until age thirty-seven, even though God had promised him the kingship many years earlier (1 Samuel 16:13). This timing confirms the importance of our waiting on God. In waiting we find renewed strength (Isaiah 40:31).

2 Samuel 5:6-25 David defeated the Jebusites in Jerusalem and took the stronghold of Zion (vv.6-8). He lived in this stronghold "and called it the city of David" (v.9). David's success resulted from God being with him (v.10). Hiram, king of Tyre, even sent men and materials and built David a house (v.11).

Old Testament History   *1 Samuel 20—2 Samuel 6*   Week Six

What made David such a wonderful leader was his ability to view life from God's perspective. He understood that God had established him as king (v.12). He also realized that God had exalted his kingdom for the sake of Israel (v.12). Wow! Wouldn't you enjoy serving under such a leader? If you desire to lead within the body of Christ, it should be clear as to how one receives such a position. Read 1 Samuel 2:7 and Psalm 75:7 for more input.

David took more wives and concubines from Jerusalem, and more offspring were born to him (vv.13-16).

When the Philistines heard that David was king, they assembled in the valley of Rephaim (vv.17-18). After inquiring of the Lord, David came to Baal-perazim and defeated them (vv.19-21). Upon receiving special instructions from the Lord, David defeated the Philistines a second time and struck them from Geba to Gezer (vv.22-25).

<u>2 Samuel 6</u> Use the maps titled *"The Journey of the Ark"* and *"General Map of Israel"* (in the Reference Section) to find the cities mentioned in this chapter. David brought the ark from Baal-judah (Kiriath-jearim) with much celebration (vv.1-5). However, it was moved by means of a cart (v.3) instead of the manner God had previously prescribed (Exodus 25:14-15; Numbers 4:15; Deuteronomy 10:8; Joshua 3:3). When the ark began to tilt (at the threshing floor of Nacon), Uzzah "took hold of it," and God struck him dead "for his irreverence" (vv.6-7). David was angry and afraid of the Lord that day (vv.8-9), so he had the ark remain at the house of Obed-edom (the Gittite) for three months (vv.10-11). When the Lord blessed Obed-edom, David had the ark "carried" (the way it should have been transported in the first place) into the city of David (vv.11-13). As it entered, David danced before the Lord, and the people enjoyed a great celebration (vv.14-15). Michal, however, despised David for his behavior (v.16). The ark was placed "inside the tent which David had pitched for it" (v.17). David then presented burnt offerings and peace offerings and "blessed the people in the name of the Lord of hosts" (vv.17-18). After receiving gifts from David, the people departed to their homes (v.19).

When David returned to his home, Michal reprimanded him for his "foolish" behavior (v.20). David defended his actions (vv.21-22), and Michal was barren to the day of her death (v.23). She was childless either because David became permanently estranged from her or because God closed her womb.

As we leave this chapter, may we desire to worship the Lord as freely as David worshipped. May we never allow worldly pressures to affect the way we praise our Creator, Friend, and Master.

Old Testament History   2 Samuel 7—2 Samuel 24   Week Seven

The History Books of the Old Testament

Week Seven

First Day

This week we will continue studying the life of David. Remain alert and glean all you can from this portion of the course. It is <u>very</u> practical, and very interesting.

<u>2 Samuel 7</u> When the Lord had given David a house, along with rest from his enemies (v.1), David lamented to Nathan (the prophet) that the Lord was without a permanent house (v.2). Nathan initially told David to do whatever he desired (v.3), but God had a different idea. The Lord revealed to David (through Nathan—v.17) that He had never lived in a permanent house (vv.4-7). He also revealed that David would be made great (vv.8-9). God would also appoint a place for His people to be permanently "planted" (v.10) and give them rest (v.11). But David would not be allowed to build the temple (God's house) because of the blood he had shed in battle (1 Chronicles 22:8; 28:2-3).

God promised David several things in 2 Samuel 7:11b-16. David would be given a house, or dynasty (v.11b). God would also raise up David's descendant and establish his kingdom (v.12). (1 Kings says that this descendant is Solomon.) Solomon, David's son through Bathsheba, would build God a house, or temple (v.13), and his throne (not Solomon) would be established forever (v.13). He would be corrected when he sinned (v.14), but God would not remove his loving kindness from Solomon (v.15). David's house (dynasty), kingdom, and throne would be established forever (v.16).

First and 2 Chronicles record many of the events included in 1 Samuel through 2 Kings. These two books also give information that is not included in 1 Samuel through 2 Kings (much the same as the four Gospels in the New Testament relate to one another), which is why we can insert Reference Point 44, *God Promises David that One of His Descendants Will Sit On His Throne Forever; Jesus Would Fulfill this Prophecy (1 Chronicles 17:10b-14)* in our time line and keep our events in chronological order. Read 1 Chronicles 17:10b-14 before going farther and see how these promises point to Christ. Write down any new insights below. Additional information follows, but before reading this material digest as much as you can from the Scriptures themselves.

Nathan related very special promises to David in 1 Chronicles 17:10b-14, many of which pertain to Jesus—his descendant (Mark 10:47). David is promised a house, or dynasty (v.10). His descendant (Jesus) is to receive a kingdom (v.11). Jesus will build God a house—the millennial temple (v.12), and his throne will be established forever (v.12). God will never remove his lovingkindness for Christ (v.13). Also, God will settle Jesus in His dynasty and kingdom forever, and Jesus' throne will be established forever (v.14). All these promises were revealed to David through Nathan (2 Samuel 7:17, 1 Chronicles 17:15).

Because the promises recorded here are unconditional, God is obligated to fulfill them. This covenant, the Davidic Covenant (as it is called), promised David an eternal person (Jesus), an eternal house (dynasty), an eternal throne, and an eternal kingdom. The eternal person (the Messiah) will sit on an eternal throne ruling over an eternal kingdom, which will give David an eternal house (dynasty). Since Jesus was first rejected by His people and nailed to a cross, He has never ruled over Israel in the sense that these verses specify. This fact proves that the Millennium (the one-thousand-year reign of Christ) must become a reality if Christ is to rule as King over Israel.

Several prophecies relate to what we have just studied. A partial listing follows: Luke 1:32-33;

Old Testament History 2 Samuel 7—2 Samuel 24 *Week Seven*

Psalm 89:3-4, 29, 34-37; Jeremiah 33:17-26.

Christ holds three different offices during three different spans of time. He functioned as a Prophet while on earth (Deuteronomy 18:15; Acts 3:22-26). He now functions as our High Priest (Hebrews 3:1; 4:14). He will, after the Second Coming, function as King (Revelation 19:11-16; 20:4). Thus, the eternal nature of David's dynasty, kingdom, and throne is a direct result of David's seed, Jesus Christ, being eternal.

Only a man endowed with extraordinary humility could speak what David spoke in verses 18-29. Here David gives God glory for His graciousness toward him and His people Israel.

2 Samuel 8 David conquered much territory during this time: the Philistines and their chief city, Gath (v.1; 1 Chronicles 18:1); Moab (v.2); Hadadezer, king of Zobah—a Syrian kingdom, which probably laid north of Damascus (vv.3-4); the Arameans of Damascus (vv.5-6). (The Arameans are Syrians.) "The Lord helped David wherever he went" (v.6), and the spoils of battle David dedicated to the Lord (vv.7-12). Even the Edomites became servants of David (vv.13-14). All of the enemies mentioned here, outside of the Philistines, lived on the east side of the Jordan.

The names of David's appointees are listed in verses 15-18, some of which should be familiar. Joab (David's nephew through his sister Zeruiah—1 Chronicles 2:13-16) served as commander of David's troops (v.16), while Zadok and Ahimelech served as priests (v.17). According to verse 17, the office of high priest was divided between Zadok and Ahimelech. But according to 1 Kings 2:26 and 1 Chronicles 15:11, Abiathar, not Ahimelech, served as priest during David's reign. Do we have a contradiction? No! Evidently Ahimelech, the son of Abiathar (1 Chronicles 18:16), took on many of the responsibilities of the priesthood, as his father grew older. Later, in 1 Kings 2:27 and 35 (after Solomon took the throne of Israel), Abiathar is totally removed and only Zadok serves as high priest, fulfilling 1 Samuel 2:31-35.

2 Samuel 9 "For Jonathan's sake," David desired to show kindness toward anyone left of Saul's household (v.1). He wanted to honor the covenant made with Jonathan (1 Samuel 18:3-4). (Review the notes on 1 Samuel 18:3-4.) Therefore, because of Jonathan, David responded favorably toward Saul's household. We entered a similar covenant with Jesus (Matthew 26:28; Mark 14:24; 1 Corinthians 11:25). Consequently, because of Jesus, God responds favorably toward us.

David asked Ziba, Saul's servant, if there was any person in Saul's household to whom he could "show the kindness of God" (vv.2-3a). Ziba told David about Jonathan's son who lived in Lo-debar (vv.3b-4). David sent for this son of Jonathan (named Mephibosheth) who approached David by falling on his face and prostrating himself (vv.5-6). David then related that he would show him kindness for the sake of Jonathan and would restore to him all the land of his grandfather Saul (v.7). Mephibosheth would also eat at David's table regularly (v.7). Mephibosheth was humbled by David's response (v.8).

Can you imagine what was going on in Mephibosheth's mind? Being the grandson of Saul, he had probably viewed David as his enemy all his days. Now he would inherit all his grandfather's possessions plus eat regularly at David's table. And how did he respond to this act of kindness? According to verse 8, he repented! He fell prostrate before David and said, "What is your servant, that you should regard a dead dog like me?" In other words, Mephibosheth realized that he deserved death. Yes, the kindness of God leads to repentance (Romans 2:4).

David then placed Ziba in charge of Mephibosheth's estate (vv.9-10) while "Mephibosheth ate at David's table as one of the king's sons" (v.11). Mephibosheth also had a son named Mica (v.12) and lived in Jerusalem with the king (v.13).

Mephibosheth reaped these blessings because of Jonathan. Do you thank God regularly for the

Old Testament History 2 Samuel 7—2 Samuel 24 Week Seven

blessings you receive because of Jesus? As a result of accepting Jesus and entering into covenant with Him, you are given life (John 3:16; Colossians 3:4) and are automatically taken into God's family. What a deal!

Second Day

<u>2 Samuel 10</u> When the king of Ammon died, David sent servants to console the king's son, Hanun (vv.1-2). Instead of receiving them in peace, he listened to unwise counsel. Hanun embarrassed David's servants by shaving off their beards and cutting off the bottoms of their garments (vv.3-4). Upon discovering what had occurred, David encouraged his servants to stay at Jericho until their beards had grown (v.5).

When the Ammonites realized they had angered David, they hired Arameans (Syrians) of Beth-rehob and Zobah, along with the king of Maacah and a thousand of his men, and the men of Tob, to war with them against Israel (v.6). David sent his entire army with Joab (his captain), and they defeated the Ammonites and their allies (vv.7-14). Joab then returned to Jerusalem (v.14). The Aramean king of Zobah, Hadadezer (2 Samuel 8:3), then called the Arameans beyond the Euphrates to join him at Helam (vv.15-16). David and his armies defeated the Arameans at Helam, causing them to make peace with Israel (vv.17-19). The Arameans no longer desired to help the sons of Ammon (v.19).

God's hand was upon David, for he defeated his foes on every side. (God so desires to empower those who walk in integrity!) However, the next chapter tells how this man of God temporarily goes astray. The swiftness, with which he loses his perspective, as well as the consequences he reaps from his disobedience, should be enough to deepen anyone's desire to avoid unfaithfulness.

Read 2 Samuel 11, which is associated with Reference Point 45, *David's Sin with Bathsheba*.

1. According to verse 1, whom was Israel fighting? Where was David? Now read verses 1-27, one of the most painful accounts in the entire word of God and let the Lord speak to you about the importance of remaining alert—especially when you are experiencing tremendous victory. Record anything that strikes you about these verses.

2. Who was Uriah? Why did David have him killed? Were you impressed with Uriah's character? Why?

3. Are you shocked that a man of God could fall so quickly? Explain. In your opinion, why would David be so susceptible to Satan's attack at this point in his life? Under what conditions are you the most susceptible to the enemy's attack?

Old Testament History   2 Samuel 7—2 Samuel 24   **Week Seven**

2 Samuel 12 After the incident with Bathsheba and Uriah, God sent Nathan to David (v.1). Upon his arrival, Nathan related a story about a poor man whose only sheep was taken by a rich man (vv.1-4). David's response has always overwhelmed me, since it confirms how quickly sin results in a loss of discernment. David, not seeing that Nathan's story related to his sin against Uriah, stated that the rich man should die (v.5). He also stated that the rich man should repay the poor man "fourfold" (v.6). Nathan then said to David, "You are the man" (v.7). Wow! Nathan's words must have rattled David at his core. Then, Nathan described all that God had done for David and said that He would have done even more had David obeyed (vv.7-8). After pointing out David's sin (v.9), Nathan stated that the sword would not depart from David's house (v.10), and that God would raise up evil against David from his own household—a family member would sexually abuse David's concubines in broad daylight (vv.11-12). Without a doubt, God exposes publicly the sin that is committed in secret (v.12).

Nathan's predictions will unfold in the next few chapters. The sword will not depart from David's house (2 Samuel 13:28-30; 1 Kings 2:23-25), family members will rebel against David (2 Samuel 15:13), and David's concubines will be sexually abused in broad daylight (2 Samuel 16:20-23). In the area of sin, we reap more than we sow, we reap later than we sow, and we reap the same thing (the same type of thing) we sow. See how Colossians 3:25 ties in here.

After Nathan exposed David's sin, David was quick to repent (v.13), and Nathan was quick to state that God had dealt with his sin (v.13). If you desire to know David's true feelings, read Psalm 51. Yes, David's sin was great, but great was his repentance, which is why he was so beloved of God. Keeping in mind the severity of his sin, read God's words concerning David in 1 Kings 9:4. Truly our God is gracious!

One of the things David reaped from his sin was the death of the child conceived through his adulterous relationship with Bathsheba (vv.14-19). However, when the child died David arose and worshipped (v.20), and returned to his home (vv.20-23), because he understood the depths of God's forgiveness (read Psalm 32:1-2). (Verse 23 confirms that children who die go to be with the Lord.)

Bathsheba bore another son (Solomon) through David (v.24). The Lord loved this child and sent word through Nathan to name him Jedidiah (v.25). Jedidiah means "beloved of God." Again, God displays his unfathomable grace!

While the previous events were occurring, Joab besieged Rabbah, the royal city of the Ammonites (vv.26-28). (Rabbah is where Uriah the Hittite lost his life—2 Samuel 11:1, 16-17.) After receiving word from Joab, David came with his own troops and captured the city (v.29). He took the king's crown, along with the spoil of the city, and placed the citizens under hard labor (vv.30-31). David overthrew all the cities of the Ammonites and returned to Jerusalem (v.31).

Even though David had sinned greatly, God continued to allow David to overthrow his enemies. What grace! But David would pay a tremendous price (in this life) for his sin. Just watch!

Third Day

Pray for wisdom and discernment as you work through today's lesson.

2 Samuel 13 David begins to reap consequences from his sin. Amnon raped his half-sister, Tamar, who was Absalom's full sister, all of whom were David's children (vv.1-14). However, after Amnon violated Tamar, he hated her even to a greater degree than he had originally loved her

Old Testament History *2 Samuel 7—2 Samuel 24* *Week Seven*

(v.15). Sexual sin outside of marriage never enhances a relationship! Amnon had Tamar removed from his presence (vv.16-19), after which Absalom took Tamar into his own personal care (v.20). David was angry over what had occurred (v.21) and should have banished Amnon for his sin (Leviticus 20:17), but failed to act on the matter. Absalom hated Amnon (v.22) enough to eventually have him killed (vv.23-29). Nathan's prophecies of 2 Samuel 12 were coming to fruition.

David discovered what had occurred (vv.30-36), so Absalom fled for three years to Geshur (vv.37-38). David longed to see Absalom (v.39), for he loved him deeply.

David is only beginning to reap from his sin. The story gets much more gruesome in the chapters ahead.

2 Samuel 14 When Joab observed David's love for Absalom (v.1), he used a woman from Tekoa to convince David of his need to have Absalom return (vv.2-20). David then had Joab bring Absalom to Jerusalem (vv.21-23), but David did not allow Absalom to see his face (v.24).

Absalom was a handsome man (v.25) and the father of four children (vv.26-27). After living two years in Jerusalem without seeing his father, Absalom had Joab approach David on his behalf (vv.28-33). David then allowed Absalom to approach him, and the king kissed his wayward son (v.33).

Read 2 Samuel 15, which is associated with Reference Point 46, *David Overthrown by His Son Absalom*.

1. How did Absalom win the hearts of the men of Israel (vv.1-6)?

2. According to verses 7-12, what role did Hebron play in Absalom's conspiracy? For whom did Absalom send in verse 12? What service had this man performed for David?

3. From David's response in verses 13-14, would you say he realized the condition of Absalom's heart? What does verse 15 communicate to you about the loyalty of David's servants? Why would you like to have an Ittai for a friend?

4. What do verses 24-29 say to you about David's faith?

5. Try to imagine how David looked and felt in verse 30. How did he cope with the situation (for help read 1 Samuel 30:6)? What has encouraged you about the way David handled adversity?

Old Testament History   2 Samuel 7—2 Samuel 24   Week Seven

6. Who was Hushai, and why did David send him to Absalom? What city did Absalom enter in verse 37?

2 Samuel 16 Ziba, the servant of Mephibosheth, came to David with supplies along with news concerning Mephibosheth (vv.1-3). (We first learned of Mephibosheth and Ziba in 2 Samuel 4:4 and 2 Samuel 9.) What Ziba told David concerning Mephibosheth (that he was elated over David's downfall and sought the throne of Israel—v.3) was a lie. Evidently Ziba told this lie for personal gain. (Mephibosheth remained faithful to David throughout David's exile.) David, however, believed Ziba and gave him all that belonged to Mephibosheth (v.4). Try to imagine how this news affected David, especially after he had responded so favorably to Mephibosheth. We must be careful to receive all the facts before judging a person's character.

As David came to Bahurim, he was met by Shimei of the family of Saul (v.5). Even though Shimei cursed David, threw stones at David and his servants, and even accused David of taking part in Saul's death (which was a lie), David did nothing to silence him (vv.5-13). David viewed the cursing as from the hand of God (vv.10-11). He also considered that God would vindicate him if the cursing were unjustified (v.12). One of the true tests of character comes when we are falsely accused. We must, as David did, wait on God and refuse to take matters into our own hands.

After Absalom and the men of Israel entered Jerusalem, Hushai, who would serve as a spy for David, deceived Absalom into believing that he had forsaken David (vv.15-19). Meanwhile Ahithophel, who previously served as David's counselor (2 Samuel 15:12), advised Absalom to have relations with David's concubines in the sight of the people (vv.20-21). Ahithophel felt this act would help Absalom politically, for the people would then realize that Absalom had made himself "odious" to his father (v.21). A tent was pitched for Absalom on the roof, and he "went in to his father's concubines in the sight of all Israel" (v.22). Thus, Nathan's prophecy of 2 Samuel 12:11-12 was fulfilled. Ahithophel's advice in all areas became the final word in Israel (v.23).

Fourth Day

2 Samuel 17 Ahithophel desired to take 12,000 men and pursue David immediately (vv.1-4). Before giving in to Ahithophel's request, Absalom sought Hushai's counsel (vv.5-6). Hushai disagreed with Ahithophel and convinced Absalom to lead Israel into battle (vv.7-14). After receiving word from Hushai, David and his people crossed the Jordan (vv.15-22). When Ahithophel saw that his counsel was rejected, he went to his home and hanged himself (V.23).

Ahithophel knew that Absalom had lost his advantage and would surely be defeated without the element of surprise. Once David regrouped, his warriors would easily defeat Absalom's forces. With David back in power, Ahithophel's life would be required of him for his role in the revolt.

Why would such a faithful man as Ahithophel turn against his lord, king David? The answer is found in 2 Samuel 11:3 and 23:34. Bathsheba was Ahithophel's granddaughter! He had let the hurt and anger from David's sin against his family make him bitter. He saw an opportunity in Absalom to exact revenge against David. And no doubt, Absalom saw an opportunity to exploit a dejected friend of his father.

David and his followers arrived at Mahanaim, and Absalom, along with the men of Israel, crossed the Jordan (v.24). (Refer to the *General Map of Israel* included in the reference materials. Remember that Mahanaim was originally Ish-bosheth's headquarters—2 Samuel 2:8-10.) Since Joab was with David, Absalom chose Amasa (David's nephew through his sister Abigail—

Old Testament History   **2 Samuel 7—2 Samuel 24**   *Week Seven*

1 Chronicles 2:13-17) to lead Israel (v.25). Absalom and Israel camped in Gilead (v.26). While at Mahanaim, different individuals brought supplies to David and his men (v.27-29).

2 Samuel 18 As David prepared his men for battle, it was suggested that David remain behind (vv.1-3). David's men loved him deeply. (Absalom only desired David's life—he did not care about what happened to David's men.) David agreed with their suggestion, but told his leaders, Joab, Abishai, and Ittai, in the hearing of all the people, to deal gently with Absalom (vv.4-5). David's men left Mahanaim and fought Israel in the forest of Ephraim (v.6). Israel was defeated (vv.7-8), and Absalom was killed by Joab and his armor bearers (vv.9-15)—even though Absalom could have been taken alive (vv.9-12). Joab totally disregarded David's command of verse 5. We will soon discover what happens in the lives of such men. An unwillingness to submit to authority eventually results in a loss of life (Proverbs 29:1).

David's men stopped pursuing Israel, after which Absalom's body was thrown into a deep pit and covered with stones (vv.16-18). Every person in Israel fled to his tent (v.17). Messengers then ran to inform David of the victory (vv.19-31), but upon hearing of Absalom's death, David mourned (vv.32-33).

Read 2 Samuel 19, which is associated with Reference Point 47, *David Regains the Throne*.

1. According to verses 1-4, how did David's servants respond to his sadness over Absalom?

2. Describe the counsel that David received from Joab (vv.5-7). How did David respond (v.8)?

3. Who was first to suggest that David return as king, Judah or Israel? What did David do in verses 11-13 that caused the men of Judah to respond as they did in verse 14? David desired to replace Joab because of his insubordination. Where did Judah gather to meet the king (v.15)? Can you remember other major events that occurred at this location?

4. Considering the events of 2 Samuel 16:5-13, would you have responded as David did in verses 16-23? Explain.

5. The truth is finally revealed concerning Mephibosheth (vv.24-30). What impresses you the most about Mephibosheth's response to David? Are you as loyal to your friends as Mephibosheth was to David? If not, how can you become such a friend?

Old Testament History *2 Samuel 7—2 Samuel 24* **Week Seven**

6. Who was Barzillai, and what had he done for David? What do these verses reveal about David's loyalty to his friends?

7. What was the source of conflict in verses 40-43?

Fifth Day

<u>2 Samuel 20</u> Sheba, a Benjamite, revolted against David and drew Israel to himself (vv.1-2). Judah remained with David (v.2). After David provided for the ten concubines sexually abused by Absalom (v.3), he sent Amasa to call the men of Judah to Jerusalem (vv.4-5). However, Amasa delayed in coming and David told Abishai to take servants and pursue Sheba (v.6). Joab, being included in the group, killed Amasa at Gibeon (vv.7-12) and continued to pursue Sheba (v.13). Finally, at Beth-maacah, the city's inhabitants threw Sheba's head over the city wall, and Joab returned to Jerusalem (vv.14-22). A very wise woman kept Joab from destroying Beth-maacah (vv.16-22)

The leaders in David's kingdom are listed in verses 23-26. Joab was over the whole army of Israel (v.23) and Zadok and Abiathar were priests (v.25). Would you have allowed Joab, who rebelled against the king's commands on different occasions, to hold such a powerful position? Maybe David disliked confronting those who refused to submit to authority (as was also the case with Absalom). Are there positive steps one can take to overcome such tendencies?

<u>2 Samuel 21</u> Because Saul killed some of the Gibeonites, God sent a famine in the land (v.1). (Israel made a covenant with the Gibeonites and agreed not to harm them—Joshua 9:16-20.) The actual account of Saul's disobedience is not recorded in God's word. David called for the Gibeonites and asked what could be done on Israel's part to make restitution (vv.2-4). The Gibeonites asked for seven men from Saul's family to hang at Gibeah of Saul (vv.5-6). David agreed to their demands (v.6), but spared Mephibosheth because of his oath with Jonathan (v.7). Again, the covenant between Jonathan and David saved Mephibosheth from physical death (review your notes on 2 Samuel 9). We too were "saved" from spiritual death because of our covenant with Christ (Matthew 26:28; Mark 14:24; 1 Corinthians 11:25). David picked two sons born to Rizpah, Saul's concubine (2 Samuel 3:7), and five of Saul's grandsons through Merab (Saul's daughter who had originally been promised to David in 1 Samuel 18:17-19), and the Gibeonites hanged them before the Lord (vv.8-9). Saul's children and grandchildren suffered because of Saul's sin. This consequence should encourage each of us to walk in obedience, especially if we have children in the flesh or spiritual children in the faith.

Rizpah guarded the bodies of the hanged men until God sent rain (v.10). David then brought the bones of Saul and Jonathan from Jabesh-gilead and buried them in Zela in the country of Benjamin (vv.11-14). David also gathered the bones of the hanged men (v.13).

The Philistines were once again at war with Israel, but after a close call (Abishai had to come to David's aid) it was suggested that David no longer enter battle (vv.15-17). Do you dread getting older and entering the "winter" of your life, or do you look forward to your "adult years"? Read Psalm 71 for encouragement. Subsequent encounters with the Philistines are mentioned in verses

Old Testament History *2 Samuel 7—2 Samuel 24* *Week Seven*

18-22.

2 Samuel 22 This chapter contains David's song to the Lord after being delivered from all his enemies, including Saul (v.1). I highly recommend that you read this chapter at your earliest convenience. Few places in Scripture state more about God's power. Verses 2-51 are basically the same as Psalm 18.

Sixth Day

2 Samuel 23 The last words of David are recorded in verses 1-7. He referred to God as "The Rock of Israel" (v.3), truly the proper way to view Him. He also refers to the covenant God made with him (v.5), which is the covenant of 2 Samuel 7:8-16 and 1 Chronicles 17:7-14.

David's mighty men are discussed in verses 8-39. These men performed heroic deeds in battle and were thus labeled "mighty men." Many of them were misfits when they initially came to David (1 Samuel 22:2). David was a leader who could inspire others to reach their full potential. Bathsheba's first husband (Uriah the Hittite) was one of these mighty men (v.39).

2 Samuel 24 David numbered Israel and Judah (v.1), but according to 1 Chronicles 21:1 Satan moved him to do it, which verifies that David had begun to put more confidence in his army than in God. My prayer is that we would never allow our achievements or what we own to squelch our trust in God. Matthew 6:19-34 is the perspective that must be reinforced on a regular basis.

Joab tried to discourage David from numbering the people (vv.2-3), but David's word prevailed (v.4). David's heart was troubled, however, after the numbering process was completed (vv.4-10). He repented of his sin (v.10), but he and the nation would reap severe consequences because of his disobedience. The prophet Gad presented David with three options (vv.11-13): (1) God would send seven years of famine; (2) the nation would flee three months before their foes; (3) three days of pestilence would overtake the land. David chose the latter because of the Lord's great mercies (v.14).

The pestilence took the lives of seventy thousand men "from Dan to Beersheba" (v.15). But as the angel of the Lord prepared to destroy Jerusalem, God stopped him by the threshing floor of Araunah (v.16). David then spoke to the Lord questioning why the nation was suffering for something he had done personally (v.17). In fact, he asked that God's wrath might come against him and his family alone (v.17). God was pleased with David's response, for Gad appeared to David and suggested he build an altar on the threshing floor of Araunah (v.18). David did so, but not before he purchased from Araunah (Ornan in 2 Chronicles 3:1) the threshing floor and the oxen for the offering (vv.19-24). When David offered the sacrifice, the plague was stayed (v.25). (The tabernacle and the altar of burnt offering were at Gibeon during this time, but David was afraid to approach it because of "the sword of the angel of the Lord"—1 Chronicles 21:28-30.) The threshing floor of Araunah is the site where David's son, Solomon, will build the temple.

You have completed your study of 2 Samuel and will begin 1 Kings next week. Review the Reference Points you have studied thus far and glance over the Reference Points relating to 1 Kings. Enjoy your day off tomorrow.

Old Testament History *1 Kings 1—15* *Week Eight*

The History Books of the Old Testament

Week Eight

First Day

First Kings covers from the latter part of David's life through the entire reign of Solomon (David's son). It also explains how and why the kingdom was divided (after Solomon's death) into the northern kingdom (Israel) and the southern kingdom (Judah). It then covers the kings of both the northern and southern kingdoms through the reigns of Ahab king of Israel and Jehoshaphat king of Judah.

Many of these kings were evil, and the spiritual health of their kingdoms suffered from their lack of leadership. When an evil king ruled, trouble brewed in the land, and the Hebrews could not prevail against their enemies. However, when a godly king reigned, God's blessing was upon the land, and Israel's enemies would fall. There is no doubt God honors faithful leadership.

Much of what is recorded in 1 and 2 Kings, along with other pertinent information, is also recorded in 1 and 2 Chronicles. To save time 1 and 2 Chronicles will not be studied in detail, but the course does require you to periodically refer to these books for additional information.

Pray for wisdom each day before you start your work. This is a necessity!

1 Kings 1:1-27 When David was old, Abishag, a beautiful Shunammite, served as his nurse (vv.1-4). Adonijah, David's son through Haggith (2 Samuel 3:4), desired to be king (vv.5-6), and Joab and Abiathar the priest supported him (v.7). (Joab, though disobedient on several occasions, had long served in David's army, while Abiathar, the only priest to escape Saul's vengeance on the priestly order at Nob, had served as David's spiritual adviser and friend.) Many, however, were against Adonijah becoming king, men like Zadok the priest, Nathan the prophet, and David's mighty men—to name a few (v.8). Adonijah offered sacrifices (v.9—evidently through Abiathar the priest), since sacrifices were traditionally offered at the crowning of a king. These offerings displayed the nation's joy over their new leader, plus confirmed that the king's power originated with God. (David knew nothing of these events.) Nathan the prophet, Benaiah, David's mighty men, nor Solomon were invited to the ceremony (v.10).

Nathan spoke with Bathsheba concerning Adonijah, which caused her to approach David (vv.11-21). (David had previously promised Bathsheba that Solomon, her son, would sit on his throne—vv.13 and 17). Nathan then approached David and confirmed Bathsheba's words concerning Adonijah (vv.22-27).

Read 1 Kings 1:28-40, which is associated with Reference Point 48, *Solomon Rules as King Over Israel and Judah.*

1. What does verse 30 communicate to you about David's commitment to his word? What benefits will we reap if we are committed to our word?

Old Testament History   1 Kings 1—15   *Week Eight*

2. Where did David tell Zadok, Nathan, and Benaiah to take Solomon? Once they arrived at this location, what were Zadok and Nathan to do to Solomon? How did the people respond once Solomon was anointed as king of Israel?

3. Try to imagine how David and Bathsheba must have felt when Solomon became king. Review 2 Samuel 7:11-17 to see what God had promised concerning Solomon. Write down any new insights below.

1 Kings 1:41-53 When Adonijah's guests heard that Solomon was king (vv.41-48), they were terrified and went their own way (v.49). Adonijah then begged for mercy and Solomon spared him (vv.50-53).

1 Kings 2 As David was dying, he encouraged Solomon to be strong and to walk in the ways of the Lord (vv.1-4). The kingdom would endure only as long as Solomon and his descendants remained obedient (v.4). They eventually departed from the ways of the Lord and were overthrown by their enemies, but David's ancestral line to the throne continues through the eternal Son, Jesus (Matthew 9:27).

David's stern counsel in verses 5-9 was for the purpose of protecting Solomon, not for personal vengeance. David advised Solomon to do away with Joab for shedding innocent blood (vv.5-6), to show kindness to Barzillai for his assistance while fleeing from Absalom (v.7; 2 Samuel 19:31-39), and to destroy Shimei for cursing him on the way to Mahanaim (vv.8-9). Joab and Shimei were a liability to Solomon, so David ordered their demise.

David died and was buried in the city of David (v.10) after reigning forty years over Israel—seven years in Hebron and thirty-three years in Jerusalem (v.11). Solomon sat on his father's throne, and God firmly established his kingdom (v.12).

When Adonijah asked that Abishag, David's nurse, might become his wife, Solomon had Benaiah kill him (vv.13-25). For Adonijah to have slept with the king's mistress would have been equal to his claiming the throne. (The severity of this situation explains why Absalom had desired to sleep with David's concubines.) Solomon also dismissed Abiathar from the priesthood (vv.26-27), the only priest to escape the massacre of the priests of Nob (1 Samuel 22:11-23). His dismissal was a continuation of the fulfillment of the Lord's words concerning Eli's household (v.26-27; 1 Samuel 2:27-36). When Joab heard what had occurred, he took hold of the horns of the altar in the tabernacle, only to meet his death at the hands of Benaiah—who was sent by Solomon (vv.28-34). Solomon then appointed Benaiah over the army and Zadok as priest (v.35). From this point no descendant of Eli would serve as priest over Israel.

Solomon advised Shimei to build a house in Jerusalem and remain in the city (v.36). If he left the city he would die (vv.37-38). After three years, Shimei departed from Jerusalem to retrieve his servants who had fled to Gath (vv.39-40). When he returned, Solomon had Benaiah kill him and "the kingdom was established in the hands of Solomon" (vv.41-46).

Second Day

1 Kings 3 Solomon married Pharaoh's daughter for political reasons (v.1), but he paid a high price

Old Testament History   *1 Kings 1—15*   *Week Eight*

for such disobedience. He will associate with foreign women, women who served gods other than the God of Israel, until he loses his passion for the God of David. Solomon and Pharaoh's daughter lived in the city of David (Jerusalem) until he finished his palace, the temple, and the wall around Jerusalem (v.1).

A high place was an elevated area where the inhabitants of the land worshipped either God or idols. Even though it was sin, the people, along with Solomon, offered sacrifices on these high places (vv.2-3; Deuteronomy 12:13-14). Solomon went to Gibeon (because the tabernacle and the altar of burnt offering were there—1 Chronicles 21:28-30; 2 Chronicles 1:3-6) and offered burnt sacrifices to God. God appeared to Solomon in a dream and asked what he desired (v.5). When Solomon asked for wisdom, instead of long life, wealth, or the life of his enemies, God gave him wisdom along with what he had not asked—riches and honor (vv.6-14). Solomon then returned to Jerusalem (where the ark of the covenant rested) and presented offerings to the Lord (v.15). The ark of the covenant and the tabernacle were in separate locations, the tabernacle at Gibeon (1 Chronicles 21:28-30; 2 Chronicles 1:3, 5-6) and the ark of the covenant at Jerusalem (v.15; 2 Chronicles 1:4).

Solomon's wisdom equipped him to settle many difficult issues among God's people. Two women came to him, each claiming to be the mother of a particular baby boy. How he solved the dilemma (vv.16-27) gave him favor in the eyes of the people (v.28).

From verse 9, Solomon viewed wisdom as the chief thing in life (also read his words in Proverbs 3:13-15). Read Proverbs 9:10 and James 1:5 to see how wisdom is attained.

1 Kings 4 Solomon was king over the entire nation of Israel (v.1), meaning that he reigned before the kingdom split. This kingdom will eventually divide into the northern kingdom (Israel) and the southern kingdom (Judah).

Solomon's officials are listed in verses 2-19. The information presented here tells that Solomon was well organized—the mark of a man of wisdom. Organization many times allows us to be more productive than we would be otherwise.

Israel (Judah and Israel together) was many in number and had reason to rejoice (v.20). Solomon, a man of wisdom, was at the helm. He collected tribute and had dominion over a broad geographical area—from the Euphrates to the border of Egypt (vv.21-24), which brought peace and security to all of God's people (v.25). Solomon also had thousands of horses for his chariots, horsemen, and an abundance of provisions (vv.26-28). God gave Solomon more wisdom than anyone on earth (vv.29-33), which caused individuals "from all peoples" to visit him (v.34).

Before you get carried away with Solomon's wealth, read Matthew 6:19-34 to bring everything into perspective.

1 Kings 5 King Hiram of Tyre, a friend of David, sent servants to Solomon after hearing that he was king (v.1). Solomon then informed Hiram of his desire to build a temple (vv.2-6). David was unable to build a temple for two reasons: (1) His involvement in numerous wars (vv.2-3); (2) He had shed blood (1 Chronicles 28:2-3). Solomon also informed Hiram that besides experiencing rest from his enemies (v.4), God had promised he would build a temple (v.5; 2 Samuel 7:12-13). He then asked if Hiram could supply the cedar since no one was skilled in cutting timber like the Sidonians (v.6).

Hiram was elated over Solomon's plan and agreed to trade cypress and cedar timber for food products (vv.7-12). Solomon's and Hiram's builders, along with the Gebalites (vv.13-18) prepared the timbers and stones for the temple.

Old Testament History *1 Kings 1—15* *Week Eight*

Third Day

Read 1 Kings 6, which is associated with Reference Point 49, *Solomon Builds the Temple.*

1. How long had Israel been out of Egypt, and how long had Solomon ruled as king, when the temple construction began? According to 2 Chronicles 3:1, on what piece of real estate was the temple erected? What had happened at this location in 2 Samuel 24?

2. If possible, read 1 Kings 6:2-38 in the Living Bible, which makes these verses easier to understand. What was the length, width, and height of the temple (a cubit is approximately 18 inches)? What does verse 7 state about the temple construction? Does God normally make a lot of noise when He is doing a great work? Explain. How long did it take Solomon to build the temple?

3. What did God promise Solomon in verses 11-13? This promise was conditional based on Solomon's obedience.

4. As you read verses 2-38, what impressed you the most about the temple? How long was it under construction? Try to imagine how it looked when all the gold was in place. Also realize that this same temple is burned to the ground in 2 Kings because the nation refused to walk with God. Take some time to review the last few Reference Points that you have studied.

1 Kings 7 King Solomon's palace is described in verses 1-12. It took thirteen years to complete this project (v.1)—it had the same outside dimensions as the tabernacle (v.2; Exodus 27:18). It was truly a magnificent structure. Verses 13-14 explain who Hiram was, and verses 15-50 communicate details of his work on the temple. After the temple was completed, Solomon placed the articles that David had dedicated in the treasuries of the temple (v.51).

1 Kings 8 The ark of the covenant was brought from the city of David to Jerusalem and placed in the most holy place (Holy of Holies) of the temple (vv.1-9). God's glory then filled the temple (vv.10-11) as it had previously filled the tabernacle (Exodus 40:34-35), which meant that God's presence now dwelt in the temple. Solomon speaks of how the Lord fulfilled His promise to David by allowing his son to build the temple (vv.12-21) and asks for further blessings on David's descendants as they sit on the throne of the kingdom (vv.22-26). He then asks that those who pray toward the temple (facing the temple) might be heard and blessed (vv.27-53). After praying this prayer, Solomon blessed the people and encouraged them to walk in God's ways (vv.54-61). Solomon and all Israel dedicated the temple and "observed the feast at that time" (vv.62-65), the

Old Testament History   1 Kings 1—15   **Week Eight**

Feast of Tabernacles. For more information on the Feast of Tabernacles, review the notes on Leviticus 23 in the study of the Pentateuch. Considering that the temple had been completed, this feast must have had special meaning in the eyes of Israel. The people returned to their tents with joy and gladness (v.66).

Fourth Day

Pray for wisdom before you start your work.

1 Kings 9 The Lord appeared again to Solomon (as He had done at Gibeon) and stated that His name, eyes, and heart would remain at the temple perpetually (vv.1-3). (Hence, the Jews had great passion for Jerusalem.)

God makes a statement concerning David that is mind boggling, "And as for you, if you will walk before Me as your father David walked, in integrity of heart and uprightness" (v.4). Wait a minute! How can God make such statements about a man who had committed murder and adultery? Simple. God honors those who call sin, "sin." David knew how to repent (Psalm 51), and, God honors such individuals. If Solomon would obey as his father had obeyed, in integrity and uprightness, God would establish his throne forever (v.5). If he and his sons disobeyed, they, along with the nation, would be driven out of Canaan and the temple destroyed (vv.6-9).

Solomon rewarded Hiram king of Tyre for his work on the temple and palace (vv.10-14), but these verses are somewhat difficult to understand. Solomon gave Hiram land instead of a cash settlement. Hiram seems unhappy with the cities and the land he was given.

Verses 15-28 discuss what Solomon built, along with his labor force. Many of the cities mentioned here are located on the map titled, *The Division of the Kingdom* in the Reference Section. (The kingdom will not actually divide until after Solomon's death, so don't let the title of this map mislead you.)

1 Kings 10 The queen of Sheba visited Solomon "to test him with difficult questions" (v.1), and was amazed with his wisdom and achievements (vv.1-13). Verses 14-29 describe Solomon's wealth, splendor, and wisdom. He was so wealthy that he "made silver as common as stones in Jerusalem" (v.27).

1 Kings 11 Considering the magnitude of Solomon's wisdom, it is amazing that only one chapter is needed for him to commit gross sin and die. What a warning for all who believe! His passion for foreign women (large numbers of them) was the weakness leading to his downfall. They turned his heart away from God (vv.1-8). He even built high places just east of Jerusalem for all sorts of detestable idols (vv.7-8). His heart was turned when he was old (v.4), many years after he had begun walking with God. Wow! Solomon's sin would result in God tearing a major portion of the kingdom from Solomon's son and giving it to his servant (vv.9-12) after Solomon's death (v.12); two tribes would be given to his son for the sake of David and Jerusalem (v.13).

The Lord raised up adversaries to Solomon—Hadad the Edomite, who had fled to Egypt when David came against Edom in 2 Samuel 8:14, and Rezon, son of Eliada, who led a marauding band of men after David succeeded against Hadadezer of Zobah in 2 Samuel 8:3-8 (vv.14-25). Jeroboam, of the tribe of Ephraim, a valiant warrior and industrious man, had rebelled against Solomon as well (vv.26-28). Ahijah the prophet approached him and prophesied that he would become the first king of the ten northern tribes of Israel after Solomon's death (vv.26-39). Solomon tried to kill Jeroboam, but he fled to Egypt until Solomon's death (v.40). Solomon died after reigning for forty years (vv.41-42), was buried in the city of David (v.43), and Rehoboam, his son, "reigned in his place" (v.43).

Old Testament History   *1 Kings 1—15*   **Week Eight**

Fifth Day

The next section of Scripture gives information relating to the division of the kingdom. The kingdom divided into the northern kingdom (Israel) and the southern kingdom (Judah). We will also study the first few kings who reigned in each kingdom.

The Reference Section contains two blank charts titled, *Kings Of The Divided Kingdom: Israel* and *Kings Of The Divided Kingdom: Judah*. Fill in these charts as we study the different kings who reigned in the divided kingdom. These charts are also presented in their completed form in the Reference Section, so you can check your work <u>after</u> you have filled in the blank charts on your own. Also use the diagram titled *The Kings of Israel & Judah* in the Reference Section.

The map titled *The Division Of The Kingdom* (in the Reference Section) will also be very helpful as you work through the remainder of First Kings.

Read 1 Kings 12:1-20, which is associated with Reference Point 50, *Kingdom Splits Into Israel (North) and Judah (South)*. Also read verses 21-33, which is associated with Reference Point 51, *The 19 Kings of the Northern Kingdom; First 12 Rulers of the Southern Kingdom (11 Kings and 1 Queen)*.

1. Which of Solomon's sons reigned after his death (refer back to 1 Kings 11:43 for assistance)? Why did Rehoboam go to Shechem (v.1)? Find Shechem on the map titled *The Division Of The Kingdom*. What did Jeroboam and Israel request of Rehoboam (vv.2-5)?

2. The counsel Rehoboam received from the elders differed from the counsel of the young men. How so? To whom did Rehoboam listen? What does verse 15 say about this turn of events?

3. How did Israel respond to Rehoboam's words (vv.16-20)?

4. What do these verses tell you about the importance of listening to mature (wise) counsel? From whom do you receive "mature" counsel? Such persons can save us much heartache!

5. What kept Rehoboam from fighting against Israel (vv.21-24)? The tribes of Judah and Benjamin (living adjacent to one another) made up the southern kingdom (v.21). However, the southern kingdom was called Judah because Judah was the larger of the two tribes. What phrase in verses 21-24 confirms that God sanctioned these events?

Old Testament History *1 Kings 1—15* **Week Eight**

6. What did Jeroboam fear (vv.25-27)? What did he consider to be the remedy (vv.28-31)? What is similar about these events and the events of Exodus 32:1-4? Find Bethel and Dan on the map titled *The Division of the Kingdom* to see why the golden calves were placed in these two locations. Why would Jeroboam refrain from using the Levites as priests (read Hebrews 7:12)? What did the Levites who had previously lived in Israel, do (2 Chronicles 11:13-17)?

7. Are you surprised that the events of verses 32-33 looked so much like the real thing? What allows you to distinguish between the counterfeit and the real? What does Hebrews 5:13-14 say about this issue?

Read 1 Kings 13, which is associated with Reference Point 51, *The 19 Kings of the Northern Kingdom; First 12 Rulers of the Southern Kingdom (11 Kings and 1 Queen)*.

1. Who came to Jeroboam? Where was he from? Where was Jeroboam standing when he came (v.1)? What did he prophesy concerning the altar (vv.2-3)? (Remember the name "Josiah," for he will be used to fulfill this prophecy in 2 Kings 23:15-20. According to God's Law, unauthorized priests were to die—Numbers 3:10)

2. How did Jeroboam respond? What happened to him? What happened to the altar (vv.4-5)? What did the prophet do for Jeroboam in verse 6?

3. Why did the prophet refuse to go to Jeroboam's home? Up to now, what has impressed you the most about this prophet?

4. After reading verses 11-19, will you listen more cautiously when someone says, "I have a word from the Lord for you"? Who told the prophet from Judah that he would be chastened for his sin (vv.20-22)? What have you learned from this situation?

Old Testament History *1 Kings 1—15* *Week Eight*

5. What happened when the prophet from Judah departed from Bethel? Where was he buried? What did the prophet from Bethel request in verse 31 and say in verse 32?

6. Did Jeroboam change his ways after these events? According to verse 34, what would Jeroboam reap for his sin? How do these consequences tie in with Colossians 3:25? In what way does this encourage you to walk in obedience?

Sixth Day

Read 1 Kings 14, which is associated with Reference Point 51.

1. Why did Jeroboam send his wife to the prophet Ahijah? (Jeroboam understood that Ahijah was a prophet because of the events of 1 Kings 11:29-39.) Verses 7-16 record the words of Ahijah concerning Jeroboam, Jeroboam's household, Jeroboam's son, and Israel. What would soon happen to Jeroboam's household (vv.10-11, 14)? (This prophecy is fulfilled in 1 Kings 15:27-30.) What would be the fate of the king's son, and why (vv.12-13)? What would Israel reap for her sin and Jeroboam's sin (vv.15-16)? This prophecy was fulfilled when Assyria overthrew the northern kingdom in 722-721 B.C. (2 Kings 17:1-18). What happened to the king's son (vv.17-18)?

2. How long did Jeroboam reign over Israel, and who reigned in his place? Fill in the blank chart titled, *Kings of the Divided Kingdom: Israel.* Also take advantage of the diagram titled *Kings of the Divided Monarchy* in the Reference Section. This resource will be very helpful throughout our study of 1 and 2 Kings. How long did Rehoboam reign over Judah? Did the nation perform evil deeds or good deeds while he was king (vv.22-24)? Take this information and fill in the blank chart titled *Kings of the Divided Kingdom: Judah.* Also take advantage of the diagram titled *The Kings of Israel & Judah* in the Reference Section.

3. Who was Shishak, and in what year of Rehoboam's reign did he come against Judah? What material possessions did he take from the land? Rehoboam replaced Solomon's shields of gold with shields of bronze. When did disobedience last force you to settle for less than God's best? Who reigned in Judah after Rehoboam?

Old Testament History *1 Kings 1—15* *Week Eight*

4. If time allows, and if you desire to study Rehoboam's life in more detail, read 2 Chronicles 10:1-12:16 and record any new insights below.

Read 1 Kings 15:1-34, which is associated with Reference Point 51.

1. Take the information about Abijam (given in verses 1-8) and fill in the chart titled *Kings of The Divided Kingdom: Judah*. (He is referred to as Abijah, instead of Abijam, in 2 Chronicles 12:16-14:1, so we can refer to him by either name.) If you have time and desire to study more about Abijam, you can read 2 Chronicles 13:1-22. Record any new insights in the space provided below.

2. What was the main thing you learned as you studied the life of Abijam? Which of David's sins is mentioned in 1 Kings 15:3-5? Can you think of other sins that David committed? The Lord refers to David as a man whose heart was "wholly devoted to the Lord his God" (v.3), even though he was not perfect in his behavior. Why should God's reference encourage us?

3. King Asa is addressed in verses 9-24. Use these verses to assist you in filling in the blank chart of the kings. List some of the righteous acts that Asa performed in verses 12-15. According to verse 17, what did king Baasha of Israel (you will study more about him later) do that caused Asa to form a treaty with Ben-hadad king of Aram, who lived in Damascus? (Use the chart titled *Kings of Syria* in the Reference Section. Also take advantage of the map titled *The Division of The Kingdom*. Ramah was in the northern portion of Judah just north of Jerusalem.) What did king Asa eventually do to Ramah? What infirmity struck Asa? Who reigned over Judah when Asa died?

4. If time allows, and if you desire to know more about king Asa, read 2 Chronicles 14-16 and answer the following questions. When facing trials, do you possess Asa's attitude of 2 Chronicles 14:11? If not, what positive steps can you take to develop such an attitude? Why was God displeased when Asa formed a treaty with the king of Aram? Why should the first statement in 2 Chronicles 16:9 motivate us to give our hearts totally to the Lord?

5. King Asa of the southern kingdom (Judah) has just died, and his son Jehoshaphat reigned in his

Old Testament History *1 Kings 1—15* *Week Eight*

place (v.24). Then, the Lord gives details of what occurred in the northern kingdom (Israel) during Asa's reign over the southern kingdom (Judah). 1 Kings 14:20 tells that Jeroboam died and that his son Nadab reigned in his place. 1 Kings 15:25 expresses the same thing plus the number of years that Nadab reigned. Verse 26 adds more information concerning Nadab. Take this information and fill in the blank chart titled *Kings of The Divided Kingdom: Israel*.

6. How did Nadab die and who reigned in his place? Take the information that relates to Baasha and fill in the blank chart of the kings. Who did Baasha kill besides Nadab (vv.29-30)? How does this activity relate to 1 Kings 14:6-11? What is the main thing you learned from today's lesson?

7. Review all the kings of the divided kingdom that you have studied up to now, and even take a stab at trying to memorize the kings of the southern kingdom. Have a wonderful day of rest tomorrow and enjoy the friendship of Jesus as you go about your day.

Old Testament History   1 Kings 16—2 Kings 4   Week Nine

The History Books of the Old Testament

Week Nine

First Day

Read 1 Kings 16, which is associated with Reference Point 51, *The 19 Kings of the Northern Kingdom; First 12 Rulers of the Southern Kingdom (11 Kings and 1 Queen)*.

1. This chapter talks about five kings of the northern kingdom (Israel): (1) Baasha; (2) Elah; (3) Zimri; (4) Omri; (5) Ahab. Fill in the blank chart titled *Kings of the Divided Kingdom: Israel* and look over the diagram titled *The Kings of Israel & Judah* in the Reference Section.

2. What happened to Baasha's household (vv.1-4)? What did Baasha do that was displeasing to the Lord (v.7)? Who was used to bring about the fulfillment of the prophecy concerning Baasha's household (vv.8-13)?

3. How did Zimri provoke the Lord (v.19)? How did Omri anger the Lord (v.26)? What common statement is made about Baasha (1 Kings 15:33-34), Zimri (1 Kings 16:19), and Omri (1 Kings 16:26)? How has studying this lesson encouraged you to become a better example to those who might follow in your footsteps? Which king was responsible for the construction of Samaria?

4. Of the five kings addressed in this chapter, who was considered the most evil? What did he do to provoke the Lord? What is stated about him (v.31) that was also stated about previous kings of Israel? Whom did he marry, and what negative impact did she have on him concerning Baal worship? (Jezebel was the daughter of Ethbaal, king of Sidon—v.31. Baal worship was prevalent in Tyre and Sidon.) What did Ahab build in Samaria (v.32)? Up to now, how many kings of the northern kingdom have walked with God?

5. Who rebuilt Jericho? What did it cost him to build the foundations and gates? How does this relate to Joshua's words in Joshua 6:26?

Old Testament History   *1 Kings 16—2 Kings 4*   *Week Nine*

6. What is the most important thing you have learned thus far from our study of the kings?

Read 1 Kings 17, which is associated with Reference Point 51.

This chapter introduces Elijah, one of the Old Testament's greatest prophets. A twentieth century Christian can learn much from his life, so enjoy yourself as we examine the heart of this man of God.

The diagram titled *The Kings of Israel & Judah* depicts that Elijah prophesied during the reign of Ahab, king of Israel. Other Old Testament prophets are also listed, as well as when they prophesied. Take advantage of this diagram frequently as we continue our study of the kings. Pray for wisdom each day as you complete your assignment.

1. Where was Elijah's homeland (v.1)? Find this area on a map included in the reference section. What did Elijah say to Ahab in verse 1? Where did the Lord tell Elijah to go in verses 2 and 3? Through what means did the Lord supply Elijah's food at the brook Cherith? When did the Lord last "supernaturally" provide for you?

2. What happened to the brook Cherith (v.7)? Where did Elijah go after departing from the brook Cherith? Who was to provide for him there (v.9)? When did the Lord last use a material need to cause you to move from one geographic location to another? What did you learn from that experience? How was it used for good in your life?

3. If you were Elijah in verses 10-12, how would you have responded (remember that this widow was to provide for Elijah—v.9)? Do "circumstances" have to look favorable initially for a matter to be "of the Lord"? When did the Lord last bless you through a situation that initially looked hopeless?

4. The widow's food supply lasted for what length of time (vv.13-16)? Why then do we worry when there "seems" to be a shortage of the things we deem to be necessities? How does Matthew 6:19-34 tie in here? What finally convinced the widow that Elijah was a man of God and that his words were truth (vv.17-24)?

Old Testament History 1 Kings 16—2 Kings 4 *Week Nine*

Second Day

Read 1 Kings 18, which is associated with Reference Point 51.

1. According to verse 1, what was Elijah to do, and what would result? How did Elijah respond to the Lord's request (v.2)? What does verse 3 tell us about Obadiah, and what righteous deed had he performed for the prophets of the Lord (v.4)?

2. What was Obadiah's concern in verses 7-14? How did Elijah convince him to approach Ahab with his message (v.15)?

3. What did Ahab say to Elijah when he saw him (v.17)? How did Elijah respond (v.18)? Ahab blamed Elijah for Israel's problems (instead of finding room for repentance). Why do those who walk outside God's will many times view the godly as troublemakers? If you have ever been perceived in this manner, were you pleased with your response to the situation? Why or why not?

4. Based on Elijah's words in verse 19, who was Ahab to assemble, and where were they to be assembled? Who ate at Jezebel's table regularly (v.19)? Remember that Jezebel who initially introduced Baal worship to Israel. What impressed you the most about Elijah in verses 20-40? Isn't our God awesome!

5. Elijah questioned the people in verse 21. Have you ever sensed the Lord asking you a similar question? How did you answer? How did the people respond after observing these events (v.39)? At what brook did Elijah kill the prophets of Baal?

Old Testament History   *1 Kings 16—2 Kings 4*   **Week Nine**

6. How many times did Elijah's servant "go back" before the Lord brought rain (vv.43-44)? Do you display this type of patience when dealing with the things of God? If not, do you desire such patience? Read James 1:2-3 to discover how patience is attained. Do you still desire it?

7. Verse 46 explains Elijah's source of authority and power. What does it say? Can a man who has God's hand on his life (such as Elijah) lose his authority and power? This question is easily answered after reading the next chapter. Verse 46 states that Elijah ran to a particular location. Find this location on one of the maps included in the reference section.

Read 1 Kings 19, which is associated with Reference Point 51.

1. How did Jezebel react when Ahab told her of Elijah's deeds (vv.1-2)? How did Elijah react when he received Jezebel's message (v.3)? Where did he go, and whom did he leave there (v.3)? This location should be familiar by now, so find it on a map in the reference section. Were you surprised that our man of God fled from Jezebel?

2. What did Elijah request of the Lord in verse 4? In your opinion, why would he have weakened so quickly? When did you last run from a "trying" situation? What had caused your weakened state?

3. After the angel provided food for Elijah (vv.5-8), where did he go (v.8)? Who visited this same mountain in the book of Exodus and fasted forty days and nights (remember too that Elijah had been fasting for forty days)? Have you ever felt as Elijah felt in verse 10? Was Elijah really the only godly man left in Israel? Read Romans 11:2-4 for more information.

4. God was not in the strong wind, the earthquake, or the fire, but in the gentle blowing (vv.11-12). What statement does that make about how God accomplishes His work?

Old Testament History *1 Kings 16—2 Kings 4* *Week Nine*

5. The Lord instructed Elijah to do specific things to three men (vv.15-16). Who were these men, and what was to be done to each man? According to verse 17, how would these men be used of the Lord? What did the Lord promise in verse 18?

6. We read about Elijah's first encounter with Elisha in verses 19-21. What was Elisha doing when Elijah first saw him, and what does it confirm about the social status of Elisha's family (remember that oxen represented wealth). What did Elijah do with his mantle when he first saw Elisha? (The mantle confirmed that God's anointing and power was upon the man who wore it.)

7. According to the last sentence in verse 21, what did Elisha do for Elijah? Had you realized that a less mature believer can "minister" to the "mature" in the faith? Why then should we ever feel inadequate when in the presence of "seasoned" men and women of God?

Third Day

Read 1 Kings 20, which is associated with Reference Point 51.

1. What king did Ahab battle in this chapter? Who won? How did Ahab displease the Lord in this situation? What judgment did the Lord place on Ahab in verse 42, and what was his response (v.43)? (Aram, or Syria, will raise much havoc with Israel.) Since Ben-hadad reigned over Aram from Damascus, Ahab evidently viewed him as a potential buffer between Israel and the powerful Assyrians. Probably for this reason he entered into a covenant with him, which confirmed again Ahab's inability to trust God as his protector and provider. Follow the order of the kings of Syria on the chart titled *Kings of Syria* in the Reference Section.

Read 1 Kings 21, which is associated with Reference Point 51.

1. What did Naboth own that Ahab desired (coveted)? Why did Naboth refuse the king's offer (vv.2-3)? What does Ahab's response (v.4) tell you about his level of maturity? (Can you believe that a grown man would act so foolishly?) Have you ever responded similarly after failing to possess what you have "coveted"?

Old Testament History *1 Kings 16—2 Kings 4* *Week Nine*

2. How did Jezebel obtain Naboth's vineyard (vv.5-16)? Do you find it strange that Jezebel took the situation into her own hands? She was the dominant partner in the marriage (this was confirmed earlier when Ahab gave in to worship Baal, Jezebel's god). Can you imagine how foolish Ahab looked while taking possession of Naboth's vineyard obtained through Jezebel's deceit (vv.15-16)?

3. What judgment was placed on Ahab and Jezebel because of their sin (vv.17-24)? (Jehu will carry out these judgments in 2 Kings 9 and 10.)

4. Just how sinful was Ahab (vv.25-26)? Who had "incited him" to respond in this manner (v.25)? How did God respond when Ahab repented? What do God's actions tell you about Him?

Fourth Day

Pray for wisdom each day before you do your study.

Read 1 Kings 22, which is associated with Reference Point 51.

1. Jehoshaphat was king over which kingdom—Judah or Israel? Who was reigning in Israel at this time? What did the king of Israel request of Jehoshaphat (v.4)? Find Ramoth-gilead on the map titled *The Division of The Kingdom* (in the Reference Section). Challenge question: Can you remember when the Hebrews first gained possession of this territory? (Hint: It occurred *before* Joshua led Israel into Canaan.)

2. What did Jehoshaphat request in verses 5-7? Was Ahab pleased with Jehoshaphat's request? Ahab's encounter with Micaiah is recorded in verses 8-28. Why did Ahab hate Micaiah? How did Micaiah's counsel differ from the "majority"? Why should Micaiah's example encourage us to stand against peer pressure?

3. What resulted when Ahab refused Micaiah's counsel and listened to the majority (vv.29-37)? Have you wondered why Jehoshaphat entered this battle after Micaiah's "gloomy" prophecy? God was not pleased with Jehoshaphat's decision (2 Chronicles 19:1-3). (Jehoshaphat's association with Ahab brought corruption into Judah when his son, Jehoram, married Athaliah, the daughter of Ahab and Jezebel.) How does 1 Kings 22:38 tie in with Elijah's prophecy of 1 Kings 21:19?

Old Testament History *1 Kings 16—2 Kings 4* *Week Nine*

4. Read verses 41-50 and fill in the blank chart titled *Kings of the Divided Kingdom: Judah*. If time allows, and if you desire to know more about Jehoshaphat, read 2 Chronicles 17-20. Why should passages like 2 Chronicles 20:12, 15, and 17 serve as an encouragement in times of distress?

5. Who reigned over Judah when Jehoshaphat died? Who reigned over Israel when Ahab died, and what type of individual was he? A king will later reign over Judah who will have the same name (Ahaziah), so make sure not to confuse the two. Fill in the blank chart titled *Kings of the Divided Kingdom: Israel* with the appropriate information from verses 51-53. Also follow these latest events on the diagram titled *The Kings of Israel & Judah* in the Reference Section.

Fifth Day

You are now ready for 2 Kings. It will pick up where 1 Kings left off and supplies information concerning the remaining kings who ruled over the northern and southern kingdoms. It will also explain how the two kingdoms crumbled. Have fun, and pray for wisdom before beginning your work.

Read 2 Kings 1, which is associated with Reference Point 51.

1. Who rebelled against Israel in verse 1 (can you remember where their territory was located)? How did Ahaziah become ill? From what source did Ahaziah desire to seek counsel concerning his illness (v.2)? (Remember that Ahab and Jezebel, Ahaziah's parents, had brought Baal worship into the northern kingdom—1 Kings 16:31-33.)

2. What did Elijah prophesy concerning Ahaziah (vv.3-4)? How did the events of verses 5-16 confirm that Elijah was a man of God? What happened to Ahaziah in verse 17? According to verses 3, 4, and 16, why did Ahaziah die? Who reigned in his place as king of Israel? Who was reigning in the southern kingdom at this time? (For more on the life of Ahaziah, read 2 Chronicles 20:35-37.) Fill in all that you can of the blank charts of the kings. (The northern and southern kingdoms each had a king named Jehoram.)

Read 2 Kings 2, which is associated with Reference Point 51.

1. What was about to occur with Elijah (v.1)? Elijah departed from a particular location in verse 1. What was the location? Who went with him? What two cities did Elijah and Elisha visit next (vv.2-4)? Who addressed Elisha in verses 3 and 5? Evidently schools existed for the prophets in

Old Testament History   *1 Kings 16—2 Kings 4*   *Week Nine*

both Bethel and Jericho (vv.3 and 5) and in Gilgal as well (2 Kings 4:38). Elijah probably traveled through these areas to encourage the prophets to stand against the teachings of Baal. What impressed you the most about Elijah and Elisha's relationship in verses 1-6?

2. What did Elijah do in verse 8, and what resulted? Who was watching (v.7)? When Elijah asked Elisha what he desired (v.9), how did Elisha respond? (In asking for a double portion of Elijah's spirit, Elisha was asking to be the successor, or heir, of the office that Elijah held as God's prophet to Israel—Deuteronomy 21:17.) What would have to occur for Elisha's request to be granted? God was responsible for granting such a blessing to Elisha, not Elijah; "You have asked a hard thing" (v.10).

3. Since chariots and horses represented superior military strength (Isaiah 31:1), the chariot of fire and horses of fire (v.11) were symbolic of God's power in battle. Thus, to comfort and encourage Elisha, God demonstrated that His power would sustain him. Describe how Elijah went to heaven. Note: Enoch was the first person to be translated (Genesis 5:21-24), making Elijah the second. Did Elisha see Elijah leave? Try to imagine how Elisha felt after Elijah's departure. What did Elisha then do with Elijah's mantle? What role had this mantle initially played in drawing Elisha to Elijah (1 Kings 19:19)? The mantle was a symbol of Elijah's prophetic office. The fact that Elisha possessed it (vv.13-14) confirmed that God's power, which had rested upon Elijah, now rested upon Elisha. What a wonderful picture of the fruit that can be borne through discipleship. Who are you discipling these days and who is discipling you?

4. Verses 15-18 can be better understood with the knowledge that the Spirit of the Lord frequently caused Elijah to disappear (1 Kings 18:12). The sons of the prophets incorrectly assumed that this disappearance was another such occurrence, but Elisha knew better. Elijah was gone. He had been translated. Like it or not, the prophets had to accept the fact that Elisha now filled Elijah's office. What were the first three miracles that Elisha performed after Elijah was translated? Considering that Jeroboam had placed a golden calf at Bethel (1 Kings 12:28-29), does the lack of respect for authority in the young men at Bethel (v.23) surprise you?

5. After visiting Bethel (vv.23-24), where did Elisha then travel (v.25)? Elisha had received much rejection since receiving Elijah's mantle. If he needed encouragement to emulate Elijah, why would he next visit Mt. Carmel (review 1 Kings 18)? Where did he go after visiting Mt. Carmel? Samaria was the capital of Israel.

Sixth Day

Read 2 Kings 3, which is associated with Reference Point 51.

1. In what year of Jehoshaphat's reign did Jehoram (son of Ahab) become king of the northern kingdom? (This information coincides with the information in 2 Kings 1:17 only by understanding

Old Testament History *1 Kings 16—2 Kings 4* *Week Nine*

that Jehoshaphat and Jehoram co-reigned in Judah. Take the information recorded about Jehoram (vv.1-3) and fill in the blank chart titled *Kings of the Divided Kingdom: Israel*. What did Jehoram "put away" (v.2)? What does verse 3 say about Jehoram in relation to Jeroboam? Do you remember which previous kings had this same statement made about them?

2. Who rebelled against the king of Israel (vv.4-5)? Where was his territory was located? (Refer to the map *The Division of the Kingdom.*) Who did Jehoram ask to assist him in fighting this enemy?

3. What crisis did "the three kings" face that caused them to consult Elisha? According to verse 14, why did Elisha consent to prophesy? According to Elisha, how would God supply the water, and what would happen to the Moabites? Did this prophecy literally happen?

4. You need to do a little homework before drawing your conclusions about verse 27. First, the word "against" can be translated "in." Therefore, "great wrath against Israel," would not necessarily be the case, but "great wrath in Israel" would be more accurate. In other words, when the king of Moab offered his oldest son as a burnt offering on the wall, great wrath came "in" Israel —Israel was furious over the king's actions! Therefore, Israel departed from the land and returned home. What did you learn from this chapter that will help you face future crises?

Read 2 Kings 4, which is associated with Reference Point 51.

1. In verses 1-7, what was the problem, and what was the remedy? When did the oil stop flowing? In your opinion, would the oil have continued to flow had they brought in more containers? What can we learn from this account?

2. Verses 8-37 record Elisha's experience with the family from Shunem. What did God do through Elisha that was similar to what He had done through Elijah in 1 Kings 17?

3. Elisha performed two more miracles in this chapter. What were they? Would you have enjoyed being Elijah or Elisha? Explain.

Old Testament History   *1 Kings 16—2 Kings 4*   **Week Nine**

You are doing great. In two more weeks we will have completed 2 Kings. Walk on!

Old Testament History 2 Kings 5—2 Kings 16 *Week Ten*

The History Books of the Old Testament

Week Ten

First Day

Read 2 Kings 5, which is associated with Reference Point 51, *The 19 Kings of the Northern Kingdom; First 12 Rulers of the Southern Kingdom (11 Kings and 1 Queen).*

1. Who was Naaman (v.1) and what was his problem? Through what source did Naaman hear of Elisha? How did King Jehoram (king of Israel) react to the letter from the king of Aram (vv.5-7)?

2. How did Elisha respond after hearing of king Jehoram's dilemma (v.8)? What did Elisha prescribe as a remedy for Naaman's illness? How did Naaman respond to Elisha's suggestion? How does verse 13 relate to what is taught in Ephesians 2:8-9 and Titus 3:5? What happened when Naaman followed Elisha's advice (v.14)?

3. How did Naaman view the Lord after he was healed (v.15)? What has the Lord used in your life to change how you view Him? Evidently a truce existed between Israel and Aram at this time. The fact that Naaman was healed and drawn to Jehovah confirms that even the most vicious enemy can become a member of God's family (through faith and repentance).

4. In what way did Gehazi disobey? Try to imagine how Gehazi felt when Elisha revealed his sin (v.26)? How do you respond when your sin is revealed? What consequences did Gehazi reap from this situation?

Read 2 Kings 6, which is associated with Reference Point 51.

1. Describe the problem the sons of the prophets faced in verse 1. (The number of prophets had increased because of the fruit borne through Elisha's prophetic ministry.) What did the sons of the prophets seek to do (v.2), and whom did they ask to go with them (v.3)? (They described themselves as Elisha's servants—meaning they were pleased that Elisha was God's man. This response was much different from the one they gave at the beginning of Elisha's ministry, 2 Kings 2.) Describe the miracle that took place in verses 4-7. Does God have to perform a miracle a day in the "physical" realm to keep you spiritually motivated, or does His word, activated through the

Old Testament History 2 Kings 5—2 Kings 16 *Week Ten*

Holy Spirit, sustain you? Only truth (not His activity in the realm of the miraculous—wonderful as it is) will sustain you over the long haul.

2. A familiar enemy returns in verse 8. Who was the enemy? According to 1 Kings 15:18, in what city did the king of Aram live? Locate this city on one of the maps in the Reference Section.

3. Why was the king of Aram angry with Elisha (vv.8-14)? What impressed you about the events recorded in verses 15-17? When did you last stand in God's power even when the enemy "seemed" to outnumber you? When did you last pray for a particular person (or persons) to see things as they really are (v.17)? Even Paul prayed in this manner in Ephesians 1:18-19. How often do you ask the Lord to open your eyes to see life as God sees life? What did Elisha's servant finally see (v.17)?

4. Upon Elisha's request, what did the Lord do to Elisha's enemies (v.18)? What did Elisha then do with his enemies (vv.19-23)? A person who does not believe in a "supernatural" God would have difficulty accepting this account. Take time to thank the Lord for giving you eyes to see. What is stated about the marauding bands of the Arameans (or Syrians) in the last sentence of verse 23?

5. The time span between the events of verses 23 and 24 is quite lengthy. Who besieged Samaria in verse 24? As you read about the famine in Samaria, try to picture the conditions within the city. The famine was a fulfillment of what God had promised much earlier concerning disobedience (Leviticus 26:26-29; Deuteronomy 28:51-53). Who did the king (king Jehoram of Israel) blame for his problems? When were you last blamed for the consequences another person reaped from his sin? Jehoram may have blamed Elisha because he had set the Arameans, or Syrians, free (instead of killing them) in verses 21-23. Who came to Elisha in verses 32-33? Some think it was king Jehoram who repented in verse 33, "Behold, this evil is from the Lord; why should I wait for it any longer"? Others disagree. However, remember, as you study the first portion of the 2 Kings 7, that the famine was lifted (in 2 Kings 7) after the events of verses 32-33.

Second Day

Read 2 Kings 7, which is associated with Reference Point 51.

1. What did Elisha predict in verses 1 and 2? What caused the Arameans (Syrians) to leave? Who discovered that they had departed?

Old Testament History   2 Kings 5—2 Kings 16   Week Ten

2. If you were one of the four lepers, facing the circumstances described in verses 3-4, how would you have responded? After studying this chapter, are you more convinced that what God says will happen, will happen? If so, explain.

Repentance and obedience bring blessing and favor, while disobedience and an unwillingness to repent result in loss of blessing and favor. This account should give each of us a greater desire to walk in righteousness.

Read 2 Kings 8, which is associated with Reference Point 51.

1. Determining the exact date of the events of verses 1-6 is difficult. Some scholars think they are a continuation of 2 Kings 4:8-37, and that they occurred prior to Naaman's healing and Gahazi's encounter with leprosy (2 Kings 5). Why did Elisha tell the Shunammite woman to leave the land? Where did she go, and how long did she stay? What occurred that caused king Jehoram (of Israel) to restore the Shunammite's land? What does this restoration teach you about God's ability to manipulate variables to supply our physical needs?

2. Establishing the chronology for the events of verses 7-15 is difficult. What city did Elisha visit in verse 7 (this city was the capitol of Aram)? Verses 7-15 depict once again Elisha's ability to discern what is in man's heart. What did Elisha see in Hazael's heart that disturbed him? What did Elisha say about Hazael in verses 12 and 13? Evidently God's commission to Elijah (1 Kings 19:15) was fulfilled here through Elisha, which was possible because Elisha received Elijah's mantle (office). Later, Hazael severely oppresses Israel, fulfilling Elisha's words of verse 12. (Follow these latest events on the chart titled *Kings of Syria* in the Reference Section.)

3. Who became king over the southern kingdom at this time besides Jehoshaphat (v.16)? What person caused Jehoram to walk "in the way of the kings of Israel"? Name other men who lived during Old Testament times who sinned against God because of a relationship with a pagan wife? What does this trend communicate to you, knowing that Baal worship was introduced to the southern kingdom through Athaliah (Jehoram's wife and Jezebel's daughter)? Take what you have studied here, read 2 Chronicles 21:1-20, and fill in the blank chart titled *Kings of the Divided Kingdom: Judah* (in the Reference Section). Why did God refrain from destroying Judah (v.19)? Press on! Today's lesson is a little long, but you should be able to finish!

Old Testament History   2 Kings 5—2 Kings 16   Week Ten

4. Who revolted against Judah and king Jehoram (vv.20-23)? Obadiah, who prophesied during this time (around 845 B.C.), spoke of how God would judge Edom for coming against her brother Jacob (Obadiah 1-21)—the Edomites were descendants of Esau, Jacob's brother. Read 2 Kings 8:24, along with 2 Chronicles 21:18-20, to find out about Jehoram's death and burial. Who reigned over the southern kingdom (Judah) after Jehoram? Take this information, along with 2 Kings 9:25-29, and fill in the blank chart titled *Kings of the Divided Kingdom: Judah* (in the Reference Section). (You may also want to read 2 Chronicles 22:1-6 for additional information.)

5. What was Ahaziah's mother's name? How was she related to Omri and Ahab, former kings of the northern kingdom (Israel)? What does this account teach you about a parent's impact on a child, or even a grandchild? With whom did Ahaziah team to fight against Hazael king of Aram, and where did the battle occur? Why did Jehoram (King of Israel) return to Jezreel?

Third Day

Read 2 Kings 9, which is associated with Reference Point 51.

1. Where did Elisha send the prophet, and what did he do once he arrived (vv.1-6)? According to verses 7 and 8, what was Jehu to do to the house of Ahab, and why? What would Ahab's family (dynasty) then have in common with the families (dynasties) of Jeroboam and Baasha (v.9; 1 Kings 15:29; 1 Kings 16:11)? What would happen to Jezebel (v.10)? (Jezebel, king Ahab's wife, introduced Baal worship to the northern kingdom. Jezebel's daughter, Athaliah, who married king Jehoram of Judah, introduced Baal worship to the southern kingdom.)

2. How did Jehu's friends respond after he had been anointed king of Israel (vv.11-13)? Why had Jehoram returned to Jezreel? In what geographic location did Jehu initially meet Jehoram and Ahaziah? What did Jehu do to Jehoram, and where did he place his body? According to verses 25 and 26, why did Jehu place Jehoram's body at this location? What did Jehu do to Ahaziah?

3. As you read about Jezebel's death (vv.30-37), what thoughts ran through your mind? Can you believe that Jezebel, at this late stage in the game, remained overly concerned with her physical appearance (v.30)? Are you "overly concerned" with your physical appearance? What steps can you take to overcome this weakness? According to 1 Samuel 16:7, with what is God concerned?

Old Testament History   *2 Kings 5—2 Kings 16*   Week Ten

4. Considering that Zimri killed king Elah of Israel (along with all his household) and took his throne, only to lose it in seven days to Omri, Jezebel's father-in-law, (1 Kings 16:8-20), why would Jezebel try to stop Jehu by saying, "Is it well, Zimri, your master's murderer" (v.31)? How did Jezebel die? What had Elijah prophesied concerning Jezebel that these series of events fulfilled?

Make sure that you have filled in as much as you can of the blank charts of the kings, and that each king studied thus far is listed there. You are doing great!

Read 2 Kings 10, which is associated with Reference Point 51.

1. Who killed the seventy male descendants of Ahab, and why? Why did the men of Jezreel choose not to make one of Ahab's descendants king? What was brought to Jehu in verses 7 and 8? Jehu proclaimed his innocence, as well as the innocence of those who decapitated Ahab's descendants (vv.9-10), because the annihilation of Ahab's family had been prophesied through Elijah (read 1 Kings 21:21-22). According to verse 11, who, else did Jehu kill? In Hosea 1:4 we find that the Lord was displeased with Jehu concerning Jezreel. Evidently, instead of being content with fulfilling God's will on the house of Ahab, Jehu became greedy, bloodthirsty, and overly ambitious. This sin brought severe consequences.

2. Who did Jehu kill in verses 12-14? How was Ahaziah related to Ahab? Why then would Jehu have been interested in doing away with the family of Ahaziah? Who did Jehu kill in verse 17?

3. How did Jehu kill the worshipers of Baal? What was done with the house of Baal (vv.26-27)? What is stated about Jehu in verse 28? What interested you most about this series of events?

4. Specific sins of Jehu are mentioned in verses 29-31. What were they? What did the Lord promise Jehu in verse 30? Remember this promise!

5. What territory did Hazael (of Aram, or Syria) take from Israel during the latter part of Jehu's reign? On which side of the Jordan was this territory located? Find it on one of the maps in the Reference Section. (Because of Jehu's sin and unwillingness to repent, God began to cut off parts of his kingdom.) Who reigned in Israel after Jehu? Fill in the portion of the blank chart of the

Old Testament History 2 Kings 5—2 Kings 16 Week Ten

kings associated with Jehu.

Fourth Day

Read 2 Kings 11, which is associated with Reference Point 51.

1. (Reading 2 Chronicles 22:10—23:21 along with this chapter would be wise.) Who was Athaliah? What did she do to the royal offspring? Who was Joash, and how was he rescued? (King Joram, in verse 2, is King Jehoram.) Where, and for how long, was Joash hidden? Note: Had Athaliah killed Joash, the line from King David to the Messiah (Jesus), would have been destroyed. Thus, Satan continues to seek to prevent the seed of Genesis 3:15, the seed that would bruise his head, from being born. And guess what? He will continue to do so until the day of Jesus' birth.

2. How long did Athaliah reign over Israel? Fill in the blank chart of the kings with this information relating to Queen Athaliah. (She is the only queen to rule over the southern kingdom.) What priest was responsible for Joash becoming king? Who commanded that Athaliah be seized and executed? (This priest was the husband of Jehosheba, King Jehoram's daughter, who rescued Joash—2 Chronicles 22:11. Jehosheba was King Jehoram's daughter, not through Athaliah, but likely through another wife.)

3. What impressed you the most about the events of verses 17-19? (With Jehu reigning in the northern kingdom, coupled with these latest developments in the southern kingdom, Baal worship was temporarily eliminated from both Israel and Judah.) How old was Joash when he became king? Imagine the degree to which Joash loved and respected Jehoiada. Jehoiada had become like a father, and Joash, young as he was, would depend on him for everything. We will continue to observe their relationship in the next chapter. Write down any new insights below.

Read 2 Kings 12, which is associated with Reference Point 51.

1. How long did Jehoash (Joash) reign over Judah? Note: There is a very good chance that Joel prophesied at this time (around 835 B.C.). How long did Joash do "right in the sight of the Lord" (v.2)? What did he fail to remove (v.3)? These high places were illegal centers where sacrifices were offered to Jehovah. (I highly recommend that you read 2 Chronicles 24 along with this chapter.)

2. What was repaired (vv.4-16)? Through what means had it been damaged (2 Chronicles 24:6-7?

Old Testament History *2 Kings 5—2 Kings 16* *Week Ten*

3. Were it not for 2 Chronicles 24:15-22, we might leave with an improper view of Jehoash (Joash). What did Joash do to provoke the Lord? What is stated about Joash in verse 22? Sin blinds, causes us to lose perspective, and makes us unappreciative of those who have helped mold our lives.

4. Who came against Jerusalem, and what did it cost Joash to have them leave (2 Kings 12:17-18; 2 Chronicles 24:23)? How does 2 Chronicles 24:24 confirm that sin brings humiliating defeat? Why did Joash's servants conspire against him and take his life (2 Chronicles 24:25)? Who reigned in his place? Take what you have learned in today's lesson and fill in the blank chart titled *Kings of the Divided Kingdom: Judah.*

5. Is 2 Kings 12:2 more meaningful now that you have studied the lives of Joash and Jehoiada? If so, why? Joash never learned to walk with Jehoiada's God (notice the word "your" in 2 Chronicles 24:5). He was content to walk with Jehoiada only. Do you ever depend on man for that which only Christ can provide? How can you make sure that those under your realm of influence are drawn to Christ alone?

Fifth Day

Read 2 Kings 13, which is associated with Reference Point 51.

1. The reigns of two more kings of the northern kingdom, Jehoahaz and Jehoash (also spelled Joash in verses 9, 13, and 25), are discussed in this chapter. Don't confuse this Joash with the Joash of chapter twelve (who reigned in Judah). Refer to the diagram titled *The Kings of Israel & Judah* in the Reference Section. What does verse 2 state about Jehoahaz? What adversary did the Lord raise up because of Jehoahaz's sin? (Use the chart titled *Kings of Syria* in the Reference Section.) How did God respond to Jehoahaz's prayer (vv.4-5)? (This deliverer will be Joash, verse 25.) According to verse 6, did Jehoahaz and Israel walk with God after His promise to send a deliverer? Take the information in verses 1-9 and fill in the chart titled *Kings of the Divided Kingdom: Israel.*

2. Who reigned over the northern kingdom after Jehoahaz? What does verse 11 say about this king? Did he live in harmony with Amaziah, king of Judah? Who reigned over the northern kingdom after Jehoash (or Joash)? Take the information in verses 10-13 and fill in the chart titled *Kings of the Divided Kingdom: Israel.*

Old Testament History *2 Kings 5—2 Kings 16* *Week Ten*

3. How is Elisha's illness described in verse 14? Who visited him (v.14)? Joash's statement, "My father, my father, the chariots of Israel and its horsemen" probably meant, "When you go, where then will Israel find the wisdom and power to overcome her enemies." (Elisha's ministry was to the northern kingdom.) According to verses 14-19, who would deliver (temporarily deliver) Israel from Aram (Syria)? What kept this deliverer from annihilating the Syrians (v.19)?

4. What happened to Elisha in verse 20? What miracle occurred in verses 20-21? God may have performed this miracle to confirm to Joash that deliverance from Aram was imminent. According to verses 22-23, why was God gracious to Israel? What does this graciousness communicate to you about God's character?

5. Who succeeded Hazael as king of Aram? What did Joash take from him? Note: In Jehoahaz's day, Aram had taken cities on the west of the Jordan other than the territory taken from King Jehu in 2 Kings 10:32-33 (on the east of the Jordan). Joash recovered all these cities. Through the providence of God, Hazael died, which weakened the Syrians, and Israel thus overthrew her archenemy.

Read 2 Kings 14, which is associated with Reference Point 51.

1. After you have read 2 Chronicles 25:1-28, fill in as much of the blank chart of the kings as you can with the information pertaining to Amaziah, king of Judah.

2. According to 2 Kings 14:3-4 and 2 Chronicles 25:2, did king Amaziah follow the Lord with his whole heart? Has a failure to follow the Lord with your "whole heart" ever cost you anything? If so, what was the cost? If you trusted Jesus to redeem your mistake, what was the result?

3. Who did Amaziah kill, and who did he spare, in 2 King 14:5? How did Deuteronomy 24:16 come into play here? According to 2 Kings 14:7 and 2 Chronicles 25:11-14, who did Amaziah defeat? What sin did Amaziah commit in 2 Chronicles 25:14? Who was sent to Amaziah, and why would Amaziah be destroyed (2 Chronicles 25:15-16)?

Old Testament History   2 Kings 5—2 Kings 16   Week Ten

4. What happened to Amaziah, and to Jerusalem, as a result of the battle between Israel and Judah (2 Kings 14:11-14)? According to verses 16, and 23-29, who reigned over the northern kingdom (Israel) after King Jehoash died? Fill in the portion of the blank chart of the kings titled *Kings of the Divided Kingdom: Israel* that is associated with the reign of Jeroboam II. The prophet Jonah prophesied at this time (v.25), as well as Amos (Amos 1:1) and Hosea (Hosea 1:1). Who reigned when Jeroboam II died (v.29)?

5. How did Amaziah (king of Judah) die (2 Kings 14:17-20)? Who reigned over Judah when Amaziah died (2 Kings 14:21-22)? Azariah is also referred to as Uzziah elsewhere in Scripture. Fill in as much as you can of the blank chart of the kings, and use the diagram titled *The Kings of Israel & Judah*.

Sixth Day

Read 2 Kings 15, which is associated with Reference Point 51.

1. Today you read about king Azariah (Uzziah) of Judah (vv.1-7). Read 2 Chronicles 26 and fill in the portion of the blank chart of the kings associated with his reign. Note: The following prophets prophesied during this period—Amos (Amos 1:1); Hosea (Hosea 1:1); Isaiah (Isaiah 1:1). Micah will begin prophesying when Uzziah dies and Jotham takes the throne (Micah 1:1). Refer to the diagram titled *The Kings of Israel & Judah* in the Reference Section and notice the names of these prophets. Why was Uzziah struck with leprosy? What took place in Uzziah's heart that caused him to disobey (2 Chronicles 26:16)? What is the most important thing you learned from the study of this man?

2. The reign of Zechariah (king of Israel) is discussed in 2 Kings 15:8-12. Take this information and fill in the blank chart of the kings. With the death of Zechariah, Jehu's dynasty ended (v.12), as had been prophesied earlier in 2 Kings 10:30.

3. The reign of Shallum (king of Israel) is discussed in verses 13-15. Take this information and fill in the blank chart of the kings. You can refer to the completed chart of the kings (located in the Reference Section) for the purpose of checking your work.

4. The reign of Menahem (king of Israel) is discussed in verses 14-22. Fill in the portion of the blank chart of the kings associated with his reign. Who came against Israel during this time, and how did Menahem respond? Pul (v.19) and Tiglath-pileser (v.29) are one and the same. (Tiglath-pileser ruled over Assyria from 745 to 727 B.C.—use the chart titled *Kings of Assyria* in the

Old Testament History 2 Kings 5—2 Kings 16 Week Ten

Reference Section.) Assyria was becoming a world power at this time, and Syria (Aram), Israel, and Judah were in decline. This Assyrian invasion was the first of three (also read 2 Kings 15:29; 17:1-6). Who reigned over Israel when Menahem died?

5. Verses 22-26 cover the reign of Pekahiah (king of Israel). Take the information given here and fill in the blank chart of the kings. Who reigned over Israel after his death?

6. The reign of Pekah (king of Israel) is discussed in verses 25-31. Take this information and fill in the blank chart of the kings. Verse 29 mentions a certain king who came against Israel. What was his name and where was he from? Who reigned over Israel after Pekah died?

7. Verses 32-38 speak of Jotham (king of Judah). Take this information (along with the information in 2 Chronicles 27) and fill in the portion of the blank chart of the kings associated with Jotham. According to 2 Chronicles 27:6, why did Jotham become mighty? Who came against Judah in 2 Kings 15:37 (make use of the charts titled *The Kings of Israel & Judah* and *Kings of Syria* in the Reference Section)? Who reigned over Judah when Jotham died?

Read 2 Kings 16, which is associated with Reference Point 51.

1. This chapter discusses the reign of Ahaz (king of Judah). You can also read 2 Chronicles 28 to find even more information concerning his reign. Use this input to complete more of the blank chart titled *Kings of the Divided Kingdom: Judah*.

2. How did king Ahaz sin against the Lord (vv.2-4; 2 Chronicles 28:2-4)? What two kings did the Lord raise up against Ahaz? Israel and Aram came against Judah for the purpose of forcing Judah to team with them against Assyria. As you will see, their plan backfired.

3. Who did king Ahaz ask to assist him (v.7)? What did king Ahaz pay Tiglath-pileser for his help? What city did Tiglath-pileser capture, and what king did he defeat and kill (v.9)? The king that Tiglath-pileser defeated ruled over what nation (2 Kings 15:37)? Damascus was the capitol of this nation. What did Tiglath-pileser do with the inhabitants of Damascus? The kingdom of Aram came to an end at this time.

Old Testament History   **2 Kings 5—2 Kings 16**   **Week Ten**

4. Do you think God was pleased with the strategy Ahaz used to overcome his enemies? What happens when we use resources that are displeasing to God for the purpose of eliminating our problems? Note: Judah will remain in submission to Assyria from now until King Hezekiah of Judah (Ahaz's son) rebels in 2 Kings 18:7.

5. What did king Ahaz see in Damascus that he desired? What was Urijah the priest instructed to do?

6. List some of the changes that took place in the temple after Ahaz returned from Damascus. What did Ahaz do to the doors of the temple (2 Chronicles 28:24)?

7. Who reigned over Judah when Ahaz died? What was the most practical thing that you learned from this chapter? Congratulate yourself for having the discipline to complete today's lesson. I realize it was somewhat long, but the Lord has, and will, honor your time.

Old Testament History *2 Kings 17—2 Kings 25* *Week Eleven*

The History Books of the Old Testament

Week Eleven

First Day

Read 2 Kings 17. Verses 1-5 are associated with Reference Point 51, *The 19 Kings of the Northern Kingdom; First 12 Rulers of the Southern Kingdom (11 Kings and 1 Queen),* and verses 6-41 are associated with Reference Point 52, *Assyria Takes the Northern Kingdom into Exile.*

1. Verses 1-6 discuss the reign of Hoshea (king of Israel). Take this information and fill in what you can of the blank chart of the kings of Israel.

2. What was the name of the Assyrian king who came against Israel (vv.3-5)? This Assyrian king (Shalmaneser V) ruled from 727 B.C. to 722 B.C., but died shortly before his successor (Sargon II) took Israel into captivity (v.6). (Use the chart titled *Kings of Assyria* in the Reference Section.) Why did Shalmaneser V have Hoshea imprisoned (v.4)? What did Sargon II do with the inhabitants of Samaria (v.6)? Verse 6 deals with Reference Point 52. From looking at Reference Point 52 (on the *60 Old Testament Reference Points*), in what year did Assyria take the northern kingdom into exile? Assyria's policy was to remove the inhabitants of conquered territories and replace them with foreigners.

3. Verses 7-18 discuss the sins that brought on Israel's fall. List at least five of these sins. Verse 15 states that Israel "followed vanity and became vain." When did you last find yourself taking on the character traits of those you were following? In your opinion, why do we imitate those to whom we are exposed (Proverbs 13:20)?

4. According to verses 19-23, what part did Jeroboam play in Israel's downfall?

5. According to verse 24, who did the king of Assyria bring to Samaria? Note: Sargon II (721-705) probably didn't repopulate Samaria. Esarhaddon (681-669) may have been the one who imported foreigners into the land (Ezra 4:2). Did these new inhabitants serve the Lord, or did they serve other gods (v.25)? What did the Lord do in response to their sin (v.25)? How did the king of Assyria then respond (vv.26-28)? How did the people respond (vv.29-41)? The people who resulted from the mixing of races were later known as the "Samaritans" and were hated by the Jews of Jesus' day (Luke 10:25-37).

This section describing the kings of the divided kingdom is one of the most difficult of the entire Old Testament. Keep your hand to the plow, never looking back. God is pleased with your progress and will reward you greatly!

Old Testament History   *2 Kings 17—2 Kings 25*   **Week Eleven**

Read 2 Kings 18, which is associated with Reference Point 53, *Kings of the Southern Kingdom After Northern Kingdom's Exile*.

1. As you begin studying the life of King Hezekiah, fill in the blank chart of the kings (of Judah). The following prophets prophesied in the days of Hezekiah: Hosea (Hosea 1:1); Isaiah (Isaiah 1:1); Micah (Micah 1:1). After reading verses 1-8, what impressed you most about this king? Did God honor Hezekiah's obedience? How does his situation tie in with Psalm 1:1-3? According to 2 Chronicles 29:3, what did King Hezekiah do to the doors of the temple? If you want a deeper understanding of Hezekiah's commitment to God, read 2 Chronicles 29-32.

2. Verses 9-12 review much of what we learned in the previous chapter. Assyria overthrew the northern kingdom and took her into exile. From verses 9 and 10, Hezekiah evidently co-reigned with his father Ahaz for fourteen years (729-715 B.C.), even though it is not indicated on the diagram titled *The Kings of Israel & Judah*. Much debate exists as to when Hezekiah began co-reigning with his father.

3. Verses 13-16 record Sennacherib's first invasion of Judah (in 701 B.C.). (Sennacherib, the son of Sargon II, ruled in Assyria from 704 to 681 B.C.—refer to chart titled *Kings of Assyria*.) Sennacherib invaded Judah for a couple of reasons: (1) Hezekiah had rebelled against Assyria in verse 7. Judah fell subject to the Assyrians during King Ahaz's reign (2 Kings 16). (2) Hezekiah had formed an alliance with Egypt (2 Kings 18:21 and 24; Isaiah 30:1-7; 31:1-3). His alliance with Egypt did him no good, for the Assyrians defeated the Egyptians and besieged Jerusalem soon afterwards. What did Hezekiah present to Sennacherib to prevent him from overthrowing Judah (vv.15-16)? Hezekiah had difficulty trusting the Lord for deliverance in this instance. He used material means to hold off the aggressor.

4. King Hezekiah's tribute pacified Sennacherib for only a short while. Verses 17-37 describe the events surrounding Sennacherib's second invasion of Judah. In your opinion, what was the most ridiculous statement that Rabshakeh made in verses 17-37? What do Proverbs 16:18 and Proverbs 29:23 teach about the proud? Soon the Lord will fulfill these principles in the life of Rabshakeh. When did Satan last try to convince you that God was insufficient to serve as your protector? If he is still trying to do so, be encouraged as you watch God supernaturally protect Hezekiah. What did you learn about Hezekiah's faith from verses 29 and 30? Hezekiah is responding differently than he responded during Sennacherib's first invasion (addressed in verses 13-16)? Yes, adversity can bring on spiritual maturity if we will but embrace it without fear.

Second Day

Read 2 Kings 19, which is associated with Reference Point 53.

1. How did King Hezekiah respond when told of Rabshakeh's words? What were the servants of Hezekiah to request of Isaiah? What did Isaiah prophesy in the presence of Hezekiah's messengers? Note: Isaiah prophesied during the reigns of Uzziah, Jotham, Ahaz, and Hezekiah,

Old Testament History *2 Kings 17—2 Kings 25* *Week Eleven*

kings of Judah—Isaiah 1:1. The events recorded here are also recorded in 2 Chronicles 32 and in Isaiah 37.

2. Why did Rabshakeh depart from Jerusalem (vv.8-9)? (Tirhakah was king of Ethiopia.) In your opinion, what was the most interesting thing about Sennacherib's letter to King Hezekiah (vv.10-13)? Sennacherib accused God of deceiving Hezekiah (v.10), which resulted in his doom. Rabshakeh desired to take Jerusalem without a fight. How can you assure yourself that your enemy takes nothing that is rightfully yours? What is your sole weapon during such times (Ephesians 6:17)? Are you understanding more fully your need for truth?

3. What did Hezekiah do after receiving Rabshakeh's letter? What impressed you most about Hezekiah's prayer (vv.15-19)? Do you give your needs to the Lord, or do you "stew" over your circumstances? How can we apply Philippians 4:6-7 during such times?

4. Why should verse 20 encourage you in your prayer life? Isaiah (inspired of the Lord) placed judgment on Sennacherib, king of Assyria (vv.20-28). Of all the things stated in these verses, what ministered to you most? How do Isaiah's words relate to the principles taught in Proverbs 21:1 and Romans 13:1?

5. According to verses 29-34, what would happen to the king of Assyria? Why did the Lord choose to defend the city of Jerusalem (v.34)? How does God's faithfulness to king David and His unconditional promises come into play here?

6. Through what means were the Assyrians defeated (v.35; 2 Chronicles 32:21; Isaiah 37:36)? How did Sennacherib (king of Assyria) respond? How did he die (also read Isaiah 37:38)? (Some twenty years passed between the time that Sennacherib returned from Judah and his death.) His assignation took place in 681 B.C., so Sennacherib ruled over Assyria from 704 to 681 B.C. (Refer to the chart in the Reference Section titled *Kings of Assyria*.) In what way were the principles of Psalm 2 fulfilled in today's lesson? Nineveh was the capitol of Assyria. Who succeeded Sennacherib as king of Assyria? This king ruled from 681 to 669 B.C. (refer to chart in the Reference Section).

Old Testament History 2 Kings 17—2 Kings 25 *Week Eleven*

Read 2 Kings 20, which is associated with Reference Point 53.

1. (Isaiah 38 deals with the events covered in 2 Kings 20.) Isaiah 38:1-6 supports that the events of 2 Kings 20 occurred *before* Assyria was driven out of Judah. Therefore, I conclude that Hezekiah's illness resulted from his forming an alliance with Egypt (Isaiah 30:1-7; 31:1-3). (Read notes on 2 Kings 18 for more details.) This alliance was sin, and the illness was the tool used of God to chasten him. (Read 2 Chronicles 32:24-26 for more insight into these events.) This chapter, therefore, is not in chronological order with the other chapters in this book. Who brought the news that Hezekiah would die (v.1)? How did Hezekiah react (vv.2-3)? What did the Lord promise Hezekiah in verses 5 and 6? What remedy did the Lord prescribe for Hezekiah's ailment (v.7)?

2. Hezekiah asked for a sign to confirm his healing and that he would be able to go to the house of the Lord on the third day. What was the sign? In the coming days we will observe what happened after Hezekiah was healed. Sometimes being healed of an illness (and having your life extended) is not always God's best.

3. A certain king sent letters and a gift to Hezekiah in verses 12-13. Who was this king, and what did Hezekiah show his officials? (This Babylonian king was the most dangerous foe of Sargon II and his son Sennacherib. Therefore, Hezekiah felt that having such a king as his ally would be good politics.) How did the prophet Isaiah respond after discovering Hezekiah's mistake? What would Babylon eventually do to the southern kingdom (Judah)? Note: Verse 18 refers to one of Hezekiah's descendants, the prophet Daniel (Daniel 1:3-7).

4. How did Hezekiah respond to Isaiah's words (v.19)? What does his response communicate to you about Hezekiah? Who reigned in Judah after Hezekiah?

Third Day

Read 2 Kings 21, which is associated with Reference Point 53.

1. Fill in the portion of the blank chart of the kings associated with Manasseh. (2 Chronicles 33 describes the events recorded here as well.)

2. How old was Manasseh when he took the throne? How many years was Hezekiah's life extended (2 Kings 20:6)? Remember that Manasseh was born after Hezekiah was healed as we watch Manasseh lead Judah into sin.

Old Testament History *2 Kings 17—2 Kings 25* *Week Eleven*

3. Manasseh's wickedness is discussed in verses 2-9 and 16. List at least five ways that Manasseh sinned.

4. The prophets pronounced judgment on the nation because of Manasseh's sin (vv.10-15). In one or two statements, describe what the prophets were saying.

5. Read 2 Chronicles 33:10-17 to get "the rest of the story." What do these verses teach you about Manasseh, and what do they teach you about your Lord? Note: After being taken to Babylon by the Assyrians (and after humbling himself), he was allowed to return to Jerusalem and reign (vv.11-13). Does this addition to the story help you better understand God's mercy and grace? Explain. The prophet Nahum prophesied during Manasseh's reign (around 654 B.C.). (Take advantage of the diagram titled *The Kings of Israel & Judah* in the Reference Section.) Nahum spoke of the eventual downfall of Nineveh, the capitol of Assyria, which occurred later in 612 B.C.)

6. Who reigned in the southern kingdom after Manasseh? Fill in the portion of the blank chart of the kings associated with his reign. How did he die? Who reigned after him? In the next chapter you will begin studying the life of Josiah, a righteous king who reigned with dignity. It should be inspiring, so get ready to be blessed.

Read 2 Kings 22, which is associated with Reference Point 53.

1. Are you remembering to pray for wisdom as you study? Fill in the blank chart of the kings (of Judah) as you study the life and reign of Josiah. How old was Josiah when he became king? How is he described in verse 2? The prophet Jeremiah prophesied in Josiah's day (Jeremiah 1:1-2), along with Zephaniah (Zephaniah 1:1). The prophet Habakkuk may have begun prophesying at this time as well (refer to the diagram titled *The Kings of Israel & Judah*).

2. Who served as high priest during the days of Josiah? What did he find in the "house of the Lord"? Just exactly what "the book of the law" was has been highly debated. I personally believe it was the Torah, the five books of the Law (Deuteronomy 31:24-26). Can you believe that the Law had been lost? Of course, considering it had been over fifty years since a godly king ruled in Judah, it is understandable how such a thing could result. What does this situation tell you about the spiritual condition of Judah? The prophet Jeremiah spoke during these days (read Jeremiah 6:10 to observe his perspective of things). Is it not amazing how quickly a nation can depart from truth?

Old Testament History 2 Kings 17—2 Kings 25 *Week Eleven*

3. What impressed you about Josiah's response to the Law (verses 11-13)?

4. Summarize what the prophetess Huldah stated concerning the future of the nation. What would happen to Josiah, and why?

5. What is the main thing you have learned from this chapter? Why should these events forever rid us of the idea of living a life of compromise and mediocrity?

Fourth Day

Read 2 Kings 23, which is associated with Reference Point 53.

1. What did Josiah do with the word of the Lord in verses 1-2? Into what did Josiah and the people enter in verse 3?

2. In verses 4-25 Josiah "cleaned house." Which of Josiah's reforms interested you most, and why? Would you like to possess Josiah's boldness? Where do you find such boldness (verse 25 might assist you in answering this question)? The events of verse 16 fulfilled 1 Kings 13:1-2. What Feast was observed in verses 21-23?

3. According to verses 26-27, why would the Lord, after all of Josiah's reforms, choose to display His wrath upon Judah? Go to the chart titled *Kings of the Divided Kingdom: Judah* and read what you recorded there concerning Manasseh.

4. How did Josiah die? If you have time, and desire more input relating to Josiah, read 2 Chronicles 34 and 35. Taking 2 Kings 23, 2 Chronicles 34 and 35, along with secular history, the events described here occurred in the following order. Nineveh, the capitol of Assyria, had been destroyed by Babylon in 612 B.C. The Assyrians regrouped at Haran (in 610 B.C.) but were soundly defeated by the Babylonians. Pharaoh Neco, fearing the Babylonians (since Neco desired that Egypt become a world power), traveled north to assist the Assyrians (2 Kings 23:29) at Carchemish. As he passed through Judah, Josiah attempted to stop him and was killed at Megiddo by Neco (609 B.C.). Take the information pertaining to Josiah and fill in the blank chart of the kings (of Judah). Who replaced Josiah as king of Judah?

5. Fill in the portion of the blank chart of the kings associated with Jehoahaz. Who made him king (he reigned in 609 B.C.)? How did he lose his position, and where did he die? Who reigned in his place, and who authorized his position of leadership? Note: Neco imprisoned Jehoahaz at Riblah and replaced him with Eliakim (Jehoiakim). Judah was then subject to the Egyptians and paid tribute to Neco. Scripture, along with secular history, reveals that Neco continued north to

Old Testament History *2 Kings 17—2 Kings 25* *Week Eleven*

Carchemish and held off the Babylonians for four years. The Babylonians, under King Nebuchadnezzar (Jeremiah 46:2), and in the first year of his reign (Jeremiah 25:1), prevailed in 605 B.C. Nebuchadnezzar defeated Neco, and Babylon became the dominant world power of that day. With the fall of Nineveh, Haran, and Carchemish, the Assyrian empire came to an end (look at the diagram titled *Kings of Assyria*). Also, fill in the blank chart of the kings (of Judah).

Fifth Day

Read 2 Kings 24, which is associated with Reference Point 53.

1. Who came against Jehoiakim, and how long did Jehoiakim serve him? With the fall of Carchemish, the Babylonians set their sights on Judah, which was the first of three Babylonian invasions that occurred over the next twenty years. At this time (606-605 B.C.) Nebuchadnezzar took Daniel, along with other intelligent and gifted youth, to Babylon (Daniel 1:1-6). Who did the Lord send against Jehoiakim after he rebelled against Nebuchadnezzar (v.2)?

2. Why did the Lord desire to remove Judah from His sight (vv.3-4)? Who was Manasseh? Who was his father? Who reigned over Judah when Jehoiakim died? (2 Chronicles 36:4-8 gives more details concerning Jehoiakim.) Take this information and fill in the blank chart of the kings. What did the king of Babylon do to the king of Egypt?

3. Verses 8-16 of 2 Kings 24, along with verses 9-10 of 2 Chronicles 36, describe the reign of Jehoiachin (597 B.C.). What did Nebuchadnezzar do at this time in Judah (this was Babylon's second invasion of Judah, the first taking place in 606-605 B.C.)? Where was Jehoiachin taken and what occurred with the people and the treasures of the temple? Read 2 Kings 25:27-30 and Jeremiah 52:31-34 for more information concerning Jehoiachin's stay in Babylon. Ezekiel also went to Babylon at this time (Ezekiel 1:1-2). Look over the diagram titled *Kings of Neo-Babylonia* in the Reference Section.

4. Who reigned in Judah after Jehoiachin, and who placed him in office? Did this king obey or disobey the king of Babylon? Also read 2 Chronicles 36:11-16 for more information. Jeremiah prophesied at this time (2 Chronicles 36:12) along with Ezekiel (Ezekiel 1:1-2)—also take advantage of the diagram titled *The Kings of Israel & Judah*. Fill in the blank chart of the kings.

5. How has studying this given you a greater desire to be a godly leader in your home and in your workplace?

Old Testament History   *2 Kings 17—2 Kings 25*   *Week Eleven*

Sixth Day

Read 2 Kings 25. Verses 1-21 are associated with Reference Point 54, *Babylon, Under Nebuchadnezzar, Destroys Jerusalem and Solomon's Temple; Takes Southern Kingdom into Exile in Babylon.*

1. What did king Nebuchadnezzar do to Jerusalem in the ninth year of Zedekiah's reign (v.1)? How long was the city under siege? What happened to Zedekiah when the Chaldeans (Babylon) took the city? What happened to his sons? Is disobedience worth the cost?

2. Verses 8-21 describe the devastation that occurred in Jerusalem. Describe briefly what happened to the temple, the city, the priests and leaders, and the people. Who was high priest at this time?

4. What class of Hebrews was allowed to stay in the land, and who was appointed as their governor? How did this governor die? Where did the governor's assassins take refuge? For more input relating to these same events, read 2 Chronicles 36:17-20a. Write down any new insights below.

Read 2 Chronicles 36:20b-23, which is associated with Reference Point 55, *Persia Overthrows Babylon.*

1. According to the last part of verse 20, along with verse 21, the Jews were servants of the king of Babylon until a more superior nation came on the scene. What nation overthrew Babylon (539-538 B.C.)? Cyrus had molded the Persians and the Medes into a great army, and this army defeated the Babylonians in 539-538 B.C. This defeat occurred only after conditions were right for the seventy years of Jeremiah 25:11-12 to be fulfilled (v.21). Note: Every seven years the land was to rest (Leviticus 25:4). Jeremiah stating that the land would rest for seventy years means that Israel had neglected this statute for 490 years (or seventy years of sabbaths).

2. In 2 Chronicles 36:22-23, what did King Cyrus of Persia desire to build? Who did he encourage to return to Canaan to carry on the work? The book of Ezra, the next book we will study, explains the events surrounding the rebuilding of the temple in Jerusalem. It should be smooth sailing from here, with Ezra, Nehemiah, and Esther finishing off the History portion of the Old Testament. They are much easier to understand than some of the previous books we have studied.

Old Testament History   *2 Kings 17—2 Kings 25*   ***Week Eleven***

3. Tomorrow, on your day off, take time to review the Reference Points covered thus far. I think you will be pleased with your progress. Only five more Reference Points to go! You are doing great!

Old Testament History   Ezra 1-6; Esther 1-10   Week Twelve

The History Books of the Old Testament

Week Twelve

First Day

The first thing you will do this week is study the relationship between the books of Ezra, Nehemiah, and Esther. Go to the Reference Section and find *Background Information for Ezra, Nehemiah, and Esther*. Read this material at least once before continuing. You will refer to this information as you work through Ezra, Nehemiah, and Esther, so it will become very familiar as we proceed.

Since we are covering Ezra, Nehemiah, and Esther in chronological order, this week we will look at the first six chapters of Ezra and follow by covering the entire book of Esther. Don't forget to pray for wisdom!

Read Ezra 1, which is associated with Reference Point 56, *Persia Allows a Remnant of the Jews to Return to Rebuild the Temple in Jerusalem*.

1. As this chapter begins, the Persians have just defeated the Babylonians (in 539-538 B.C.). In what year of Cyrus' reign did the events of this chapter take place? Some debate exists as to when Cyrus began his reign. Some scholars think he took the throne in 539-538, while others view his reign beginning in 536 B.C., two years after Persia overthrew Babylon. Why did the Lord stir Cyrus' spirit? For more input concerning Jeremiah's prophecy, read Jeremiah 25:11-12? In Cyrus' opinion, what had the Lord "appointed" him to do (v.2)? What had Isaiah stated about Cyrus almost two hundred years earlier (Isaiah 44:28-45:7)? The temple (built in the book of Ezra) was completed in 516 B.C., exactly seventy years after being destroyed in 586 B.C. Thus, one way to calculate Jeremiah's 70 years (of Jeremiah 25:11-12) is from the destruction of King Solomon's temple (in 586 B.C.) to the completion of the temple in the book of Ezra (in 516 B.C.). Also, if Cyrus did begin reigning in 536, the time from the first deportation of Jews from Jerusalem (in 606-605 B.C.) to Cyrus' first year as ruler of Persia (536 B.C.) is 70 years. (According to Josephus, a Jewish historian, Cyrus allowed the Jews to return to Jerusalem after hearing Isaiah 44:24-28 read by the prophet Daniel.) Cyrus never knew the Lord—Isaiah 45:4-5.

2. According to verse 3, who was allowed to return to Jerusalem, and what were they to do upon arrival? Unlike the Assyrians and Babylonians, who uprooted their captives, Persia allow a conquered people to remain and maintain the religious, political, and social climate within their land. Persia believed that a happy people were less likely to rebel. Use the information in the Reference Section titled "*Background Information for Ezra, Nehemiah, and Esther*." Can you imagine how the Jews must have felt!? God had done the impossible, and they were now free to return to their homeland. When was the last time the Lord did the "impossible" for you?

3. Verse 5 lists the people who would return to rebuild the temple. Who were they, and what role did the Lord play in all of this? Those who were to return to Jerusalem had material needs. How

Old Testament History   Ezra 1-6; Esther 1-10   **Week Twelve**

were those needs met (v.6)?

4. What did King Cyrus contribute to the "cause"? What had king Nebuchadnezzar done with these articles? How would you have felt had you been responsible for protecting these articles (very valuable articles) over such a long journey (approximately 4 months)? Sheshbazzar (v.8) is Zerubbabel.

Ezra 2 The Jews who returned to Jerusalem with Zerubbabel and Jeshua are listed in verses 1-67. After arriving in Jerusalem, the heads of the father's households contributed willingly toward the building of the temple (vv.68-69). The priests, Levites, and all the Israelites settled in their own cities (v.70).

Ezra 3 The Jews first build the altar of burnt offering and began offering sacrifices to the Lord (vv.1-6). They then hired laborers and purchased materials for the work of the temple (v.7). In the second month of the second year after arriving in Jerusalem, Zerubbabel, Jeshua, along with all involved in the work, began building the house of the Lord (vv.8-9). Jeshua (Joshua) was the high priest, and Zerubbabel was governor of Judah (read Haggai 1:1 and Zechariah 6:11). Also read 1 Chronicles 3:17-19 to discover that Zerubbabel was the grandson of King Jehoiachin (or Jeconiah) of Judah (Jehoiachin was taken into exile in 597 B.C. by the Babylonians). After completing the foundation (v.10), the priests and Levites sang praises to God and the people shouted (vv.10-11). However, some who had seen the previous temple (King Solomon's temple) wept because of the inferiority of this second temple (vv.12-13; Haggai 2:3).

Second Day

Ezra 4 When the enemies of those who returned from exile heard that the temple was being rebuilt, they asked that they might assist in the work (vv.1-2). These enemies had been in the land since the days of Esarhaddon king of Assyria (v.2), who ruled from 680 to 668 B.C. Because they were not pure Jews (because of what occurred in 2 Kings 17:24-41) their offer was refused (v.3). (Zerubbabel and Jeshua responded wisely here, for if the Jewish race was to remain a separate race, the bloodlines had to remain pure.) After being rejected, these same enemies tried to frustrate the work (vv.4-5).

Verses 6-23 can be viewed as a parenthetical expression, for they actually occur at a later date. Because verse 6 takes place during the reign of Ahasuerus (or Xerxes—486-464 B.C.), it belongs chronologically between chapters 6 and 7 of the book of Ezra. (Look over the chart titled *Chronology of the Persian Kings* in the Reference Section along with what is included in *Background Information for Ezra, Nehemiah, and Esther*.) Ahasuerus (Xerxes) was the Persian king who ruled during the days of Queen Esther.

The events of verses 7-23 occurred during the reign of Artaxerxes (who reigned in 464-423 B.C.). Read what is written about Artaxerxes in *Background Information for Ezra, Nehemiah, and Esther* in the Reference Section. The temple had already been completed (in 516 B.C.) before these events occurred, for the building of the wall is the concern here, not the temple.

Verse 24 fits with verse 5 of this chapter. Thus, the work on the house of the Lord ceased after the

Old Testament History   Ezra 1-6; Esther 1-10   **Week Twelve**

events of verses 1-5.

Ezra 5 Through the encouragement of the prophets Haggai and Zechariah the work on the temple resumed (vv.1-2). Note: No work had been done for approximately 15 years—since shortly after the foundation had been laid in the second year of their coming to Jerusalem. Both Haggai and Zechariah began prophesying in the second year of King Darius I (Haggai 1:1, Zechariah 1:1), who began reigning in 522 B.C. (making it 520 B.C. when the work on the temple resumed). Tattenai ("the governor of the province beyond the river"—the Euphrates River), Shethar-bozenai, along with their colleagues, questioned if a decree had been issued to rebuild the temple (v.3). The Jews did not stop when confronted with this question, but were determined to work until a reply was received from Darius. Verses 6-17 record the letter that Tattenai and his colleagues sent to King Darius.

Ezra 6 After receiving Tattenai's letter, King Darius issued a decree and a search was made concerning King Cyrus' decree (vv.1-5). The decree was found, and Darius ordered Tattenai, Shethar-bozenai, and their colleagues to do nothing to hinder the work (vv.6-7). The price of the entire expense of the temple was to be paid from the royal treasury (v.8). Darius even ordered that the sacrifices be purchased with moneys from the royal treasury and that the priests "pray for the life of the king and his sons" (vv.9-10). Absolutely no one was to violate this decree (vv.11-12).

Tattenai, Shethar-bozenai, and his colleagues carried out Darius' decree, and the temple was completed in the sixth year of the reign of King Darius (vv.13-15), in 516 B.C., four years after Haggai and Zechariah began encouraging the people. Therefore, it was completed 70 years after being destroyed (it was destroyed in 586 B.C.). If Jeremiah's prophecy of 70 years (Jeremiah 25:11-12) was pointing to the destruction and rebuilding of the temple, it was fulfilled to the very year. The temple was dedicated with great celebration (vv.16-18), and the Passover and Feast of Unleavened Bread were observed at their appointed times (vv.19-22).

Third Day

To understand how the book of Esther fits into the scheme of things, you should review the information in the Reference Section titled *Background Information for Ezra, Nehemiah, and Esther*. Refer there as needed. Remember to pray for wisdom! If possible, read every word of this book. It is one of the most fascinating stories in the entire word of God.

Esther 1 The events of Esther take place in the days of Ahasuerus (or Xerxes) king of Persia (v.1). He reigned from 486 to 464 B.C. (refer to *Background Information for Ezra, Nehemiah, and Esther*) from Susa the capital (v.2). In the third year of his reign (v.3—in 483 B.C.) he gave a banquet and requested that Queen Vashti be brought before him for the purpose of displaying her beauty (vv.3-11). When she refused to appear, she was no longer allowed in the king's presence (vv.12-22).

Esther 2 Someone suggested to the king that a beautiful young virgin be found to replace Vashti (vv.1-4). A Jew named Mordecai living in Susa the capitol had been exiled (in 597 B.C.) with King Jeconiah (King Jehoiachin). He was of the tribe of Benjamin and had raised his uncle's daughter, Esther, a beautiful Jewish virgin (vv.5-7). Esther was chosen by King Ahasuerus to replace Vashti (vv.8-18), but she, upon Mordecai's request, did not reveal her Jewishness (v.10). Mordecai discovered a plot against the king, reported it to Queen Esther, who reported it to the king, and both offenders were hanged on gallows (vv.19-23). Mordecai's act of kindness "was written in the Book of the Chronicles in the king's presence" (v.23).

Esther 3 After this latest plot against the king, King Ahasuerus elevated Haman to a position of

Old Testament History   *Ezra 1-6; Esther 1-10*   *Week Twelve*

power in the Persian kingdom (v.1). All the king's servants at the king's gate bowed and paid homage to Haman except for Mordecai (v.2). (The king had commanded that they bow—v.2.) Haman desired to do away with Mordecai and all like him who were of Jewish decent. He even obtained an edict from King Ahasuerus to exterminate the Jews (vv.6-15), which was to be accomplished on the thirteenth day of the first month. (No one but Mordecai knew that Queen Ester was a Jew. This was also an attempt by Satan to prevent the Messiah, the seed of Genesis 3:15, and a Jew, from being born.)

Fourth Day

Esther 4 A great concern arose over this edict among Mordecai and the Jews (vv.1-3). Mordecai sent word through Hathach, Esther's servant, to have Esther approach King Ahasuerus on behalf of the Jews (vv.4-8). Esther's reply to Mordecai (through Hathach) was that no one approached the king unless he had been summoned. In fact, to approach his presence before being asked meant certain death (vv.9-12). Mordecai's message and response to Esther was awesome! He said (v.14), "For if you remain silent at this time, relief and deliverance will arise from the Jews from another place and you and your father's house will perish. And who knows whether you have not attained royalty for such a time as this?" Mordecai understood that all authority, be it kings, queens, or whatever, is ordained of the Lord. (Paul addressed this in Romans 13:1.) Mordecai also realized that deliverance would come through some means because of God's unconditional promises to the Jews. They were His people, and the Messiah had to be born a Jew. For this reason, Mordecai could speak with such boldness. Esther responded with these famous words, "If I perish, I perish," but not before requesting that Mordecai have the Jews in Susa fast for her (vv.15-16). Mordecai did so (v.17) and God honors Esther's obedience.

Esther 5 When Queen Esther approached King Ahasuerus, "she obtained favor in his sight" (vv.1-2). Isn't it interesting how Proverbs 21:1 applies here? God does amazing things when His people fast and pray! The king told Esther to request anything she desired, even half the kingdom (v.3). Esther requested that the king and Haman come to a banquet that she would prepare (vv.4-8). This caused Haman to become even more conceited—for he alone, outside of the king and queen, had been invited (vv.9-12). However, the fact that Mordecai would not bow hindered Haman from enjoying any of his latest "good fortune" (v.13). Zeresh, Haman's wife, suggested that he have gallows built, have the king hang Mordecai, and then be off to enjoy the banquet (v.14). Haman had the gallows built (v.14), which sets the stage for one of the most intriguing incidents in the entire Old Testament. Hang on as God humbles the proud and supernaturally delivers His own.

Esther 6 The king had difficulty sleeping the night before the banquet, so he had the chronicles of the kingdom read before him (v.1). Upon discovering Mordecai's act of kindness (of Esther 2:21-22), the king decided to honor Mordecai (vv.2-3). Haman, who was entering the court to request that the king hang Mordecai (v.4), was asked what should be done for the person the king desired to honor (vv.5-6). Haman, thinking it was he who would be honored, suggested that this person wear one of the king's royal robes, ride on the king's horse, and that one of the king's most noble princes lead the horse through the city square proclaiming this man was to be honored (vv.7-9). And now for the climax of our story! King Ahasuerus commands Haman to do all that he had suggested (v.10). Haman arrayed Mordecai in the king's robe and lead him on horseback through the city square proclaiming, "Thus it shall be done to the man whom the king desires to honor" (v.11). Wow! Haman returned home "mourning, with his head covered" (v.12). After reporting to his wife and friends what had occurred, they proclaim that Haman would fall before Mordecai (v.13). Wow! Isn't it interesting how fast unfaithful friends will turn on you? The king's eunuchs then brought Haman to the banquet (v.14).

Old Testament History   Ezra 1-6; Esther 1-10   *Week Twelve*

Fifth Day

Esther 7 At the banquet, King Ahasuerus asked that Esther make a request (vv.1-2—any request would be granted her up to half the kingdom). Esther asked that the Jews might be spared and informed the king of Haman's plot (vv.3-6). The king responded by hanging Haman on the gallows that Haman had prepared for Mordecai (vv.7-10).

Esther 8 Mordecai was brought to the king and given the king's signet ring which had been in Haman's possession (vv.1-2). Mordecai was also placed over Haman's house (v.2). Esther then asked that a letter be written to save the Jews in the king's provinces (vv.3-6). The king responded by giving Esther and Mordecai the authority to write such a letter and seal it with his signet ring (vv.7-8). Through Mordecai's letter, authority was given to all Jews in the king's provinces to protect themselves on the thirteenth day of the twelfth month (vv.9-12). The letter was then delivered to the people (vv.12-14). Mordecai and the Jews were granted favor in the kingdom, in fact, many people in the king's 127 provinces became Jews (vv.15-17). God can use adversity to draw the lost to Himself.

Sixth Day

Esther 9 The Jews killed their enemies throughout the king's provinces on the thirteenth day of the twelfth month, including the ten sons of Haman (vv.1-10, 16-19). Even the king's assistants aided the Jews because of Mordecai's greatness (vv.3-4). On the next day (on the fourteenth day of the twelfth month), Haman's ten dead sons were hanged at the request of Queen Esther, and the Jews destroyed an additional three hundred enemies in Susa (vv.11-14). Note: They took no plunder (vv.10 and 16) even though King Ahasuerus had granted them permission to do so (Esther 8:11). Mordecai sent a letter to all the provinces of King Ahasuerus (v.20) making the fourteenth and fifteenth days of the twelfth month holidays (vv.21-28). These holidays were to be called Purim (v.26). Queen Esther, along with Mordecai, wrote an additional letter confirming these two days as Purim (vv.29-32).

Esther 10 The author ends this book speaking of Mordecai's power, favor, and compassion. Mordecai was superseded in power only by the king, was granted favor with the Jews, and was "one who sought the good of his people and one who spoke for the welfare of his whole nation" (vv.1-3). May we all be as faithful as Mordecai!

Next week we will finish the book of Ezra and look at the entire book of Nehemiah. It should be fun! You will then have completed your study of the History portion of the Old Testament. You should be pleased with your progress. You can rest assured that the Lord is pleased. In fact, He is probably grinning from ear to ear, eagerly awaiting the opportunity to change all you have learned to revelation!!

Old Testament History *Ezra 7-10; Nehemiah 1-13* *Week Thirteen*

The History Books of the Old Testament

Week Thirteen

First Day

The events recorded in the book of Esther occurred during the 58 years between Ezra 6 and Ezra 7. In Ezra 7 and 8, Ezra arrives in Jerusalem (in 457 B.C.) to teach the Law, to beautify the temple, and to restore the order of worship in the temple. Look over the *Background Information for Ezra, Nehemiah, and Esther* in the Reference Section.

Ezra 7 Artaxerxes continued to reign in Persia (v.1); he reigned from 464 to 423 B.C. He allowed Ezra, "a scribe skilled in the law of Moses" (v.6), to leave Babylon and travel to Jerusalem (vv.1-8). (Ezra was also a priest, being a descendant of the priestly line—vv.1-5, 12.) Because God's hand was upon Ezra, King Artaxerxes granted him everything he requested (v.6). Even priests, Levites, singers, gatekeepers, and temple servants were allowed to accompany Ezra (v.7). Ezra and his companions departed from Babylon on the first month of the seventh year of King Artaxerxes' reign and arrived in Jerusalem four months later (vv.8-9). It took them four months to travel nine hundred miles. Ezra and his companions arrived in Jerusalem in 457 B.C.

Special attention should be given to the last phrase in verses 9 and all of verse 10. "The good hand of his God was upon him. For Ezra had set his heart to study the law of the Lord, and to practice it, and to teach His statutes and ordinances in Israel" (v.10). Wow! Have you "set your heart" to study God's word? A major difference lies between having a nominal hunger for God's word and "setting your heart." A person who sets his heart bases the decisions he makes on how it will affect his time in God's word (and his time in prayer). He never considers doing anything without first asking, "Will the time expended in this endeavor help or hinder in my pursuit of God's heart?" Of course, to know truth without applying it on a consistent basis is an act of futility. Consequently, Ezra received God's favor because he not only knew truth, but also lived it and taught it as well (v.10). May we be so blessed as to reap the benefit of practicing God's truth.

Verses 11-26 record a copy of King Artaxerxes' decree issued on Ezra's behalf. If you desire to see how God's word, anointed by the Spirit of God, can bring favor, read these passages. Ezra had become "learned in the words of the commandments of the Lord and His statutes to Israel" (v.11). As a result, Artaxerxes observed Ezra's integrity, purity, godliness, and trustworthiness. Consequently, Artaxerxes arranged for anything and everything Ezra would need. Wow! Ezra understood that God had brought this about and blessed the Lord (27-28). He gathered men with leadership qualities to go with him (v.28).

Ezra 8 Verses 1-14 list the men who were to accompany Ezra to Jerusalem. After assembling these men, Ezra found no Levites among them (v.15). Arrangements were made and Levites were gathered (vv.16-20). Things were now set for the journey.

Ezra proclaimed a fast to seek God's blessings for the journey (v.21). Ezra was ashamed to ask for troops and horsemen since he had boasted (to the king) concerning God's favor toward the righteous (v.22). The Lord listened to their concerns (v.23) and all was well.

Ezra assigned twelve of the leading priests to care for the silver, gold, and utensils to be carried to Jerusalem (vv.24-30). The Lord protected Ezra and his fellow travelers (v.31) and they arrived safely in Jerusalem (v.32). After three days (v.32), the silver, gold, and utensils were weighed in the temple and the weights recorded (vv.33-34). Burnt sacrifices were offered to the Lord, and King Artaxerxes' edicts were presented to the king's satraps and governors, resulting in support for

Old Testament History   *Ezra 7-10; Nehemiah 1-13*   *Week Thirteen*

the Jews and the house of the Lord (vv.35-36).

Ezra 9 Soon after arriving in Jerusalem, Ezra discovered that some of the Jews who had come with Zerubbabel and Jeshua (the Jews who had rebuilt the temple) had married foreign women (vv.1-2). Ezra was appalled to the point of tearing his clothes and pulling out hair from his head and beard (v.3). All who were concerned over the matter then gathered with Ezra (v.4). The chapter ends with Ezra's prayer of repentance for the nation (vv.5-15)—and what a prayer it was! Ezra realized the price of sin. Can you believe how sensitive the word of God had made him to sin?

Second Day

Ezra 10 Many people gathered to Ezra and encouraged him to have the people put away their foreign wives (vv.1-4). Ezra then sent a proclamation to all Israel that they should gather in Jerusalem (vv.5-8). The men of Benjamin and Judah assembled in Jerusalem in the ninth month (meaning that Ezra had been in the land around four months—v.9; Ezra 7:8). Ezra encouraged all offenders to separate themselves from their foreign wives (vv.10-11); the men agreed (vv.12-15). Ezra selected leaders to investigate the matter (v.16), and after two months of research (vv.16-17) all who had married foreign women were listed (vv.18-44).

You have just completed your study of the book of Ezra. You might want to review the Reference Points studied thus far before continuing.

Over the next five days we will do an overview of Nehemiah. Don't be discouraged, for it is much easier than some of the books you have already mastered.

Before Nehemiah came on the scene, the temple had been rebuilt (Ezra 1-6), and Ezra had returned to Jerusalem (Ezra 7-10). In fact, Nehemiah came to Jerusalem approximately 13 years after Ezra and almost 100 years after Zerubbabel and Jeshua. God was calling Nehemiah to rebuild the wall of the city. The temple had been completed (in 516 B.C.), but no wall existed for its protection. This book explains how God honored Nehemiah's faith, diligence, and perseverance. Use the *Background Information for Ezra, Nehemiah, and Esther* (in the Reference Section) as you complete this week's material.

Nehemiah 1 In the twentieth year of King Artaxerxes I, while Nehemiah was at Susa the capitol (v.1), Nehemiah heard of the distress in Jerusalem (vv.2-3). Hanani, one of Nehemiah's blood relatives, along with other men from Judah, gave this report to Nehemiah (v.2). The wall in Jerusalem had been broken down and its gates were burned with fire (v.3). To understand what was occurring here, we need to review our notes on Ezra 4:7-23.

King Artaxerxes I is first addressed in Ezra 4:7-23. In verses 7-16, Rehum the commander, and Shimshai the scribe, informed Artaxerxes I that the Jews were rebuilding Jerusalem. The Temple was not the issue here, for it had already been completed under the reign of Darius I in 516 B.C. The city was the concern (v.16). Artaxerxes I responded to Rehum, Shimshai, and their colleagues, telling them to issue a decree so the work on the city might cease (v.17-22). The work could be resumed only if King Artaxerxes I issued a decree (v.21). In verse 23, the enemies of the Jews (Rehum, Shimshai, and their colleagues) stopped the work by force and broke down part of the wall (Nehemiah 1:3-4). This destruction probably occurred in 446 B.C. and may have partially resulted from Israel's sin of marrying foreign women (Ezra 9-10). The destruction of the wall in 446 B.C., rather than the destruction of 586 B.C. (at the hands of the Babylonians), was the issue in Nehemiah 1:3.

This news overwhelmed Nehemiah (vv.4-11). He brought the nation's sins before God (vv.4-10) and asked that he might be granted favor with King Artaxerxes I (v.11).

Old Testament History   *Ezra 7-10; Nehemiah 1-13*   **Week Thirteen**

Read Nehemiah 2. Verses 1-8 of this chapter are associated with Reference Point 57, *Persia Allows Nehemiah to Rebuild the Wall Around Jerusalem.*

1. What king was ruling in Persia at this time? You can use *Background Information for Ezra, Nehemiah, and Esther* (in the Reference Section) to follow these latest developments. What had caused Nehemiah's sadness?

2. What did Nehemiah ask of the king (v.5)? How did the king respond (v.6)? How did Nehemiah respond to the king's question (v.6)? Nehemiah gave the king a definite time (v.6). What does his response tell you about Nehemiah? Are you a person who plans ahead and has good answers for tough questions? If not, what can you do if you desire to become such a person?

3. What did Nehemiah request of the king (vv.7-8)? How did king Artaxerxes I respond in the latter part of verse 8? Remember this decree! It was issued in 445 B.C. for the rebuilding of the wall in Jerusalem.

Nehemiah 2:9-20 Nehemiah and the king's escort, arrived in Jerusalem (v.9). Sanballat and Tobiah (enemies of the Jews) were very upset that someone had come to "seek the welfare of the sons of Israel" (v.10). After having been in Jerusalem for three days (v.11), Nehemiah inspected the wall of the city by night (vv.12-16). At this stage, Nehemiah had informed no one of his plans (vv.12 and 16). After the inspection was completed, he encouraged the people to "arise and build" (vv.17-18). The people did so (v.18), but Sanballat, Tobiah, and Geshem mocked them and accused them of rebelling against the king (v.19). Nehemiah responded that God would give the Jews success (v.20). After all, these enemies had no "portion, right, or memorial in Jerusalem" (v.20).

Third Day

Nehemiah 3 describes how the wall and gates were repaired. This work required a joint effort since different groups were responsible for different sections of the wall. Have you wondered what would occur if the body of Christ had such unity?

Nehemiah 4 Sanballat and Tobiah mocked the Jews, ridiculing their work before their friends "and the wealthy men of Samaria" (vv.1-3). How could these Jews rebuild the wall with "stones from the dusty rubble even the burned ones" (v.2)? Nehemiah prayed (v.4), for their words had "demoralized the builders" (v.5). However, the wall was built to half its height (v.6).

When the enemies of the Jews heard that the work continued, they were angered (v.7) and conspired to cause a disturbance in Jerusalem (v.8). (Even today our enemy attempts to raise up disturbances to prevent us from accomplishing our goals.) Nehemiah and the people prayed and set up a guard against the enemy (vv.9-23). Some people even worked with one hand while holding their weapon in the other (v.17).

Nehemiah 5 Verses 1-13 describe the economic problems facing the Jews. These passages also explain Nehemiah's remedy. The Jewish nobles and rulers were taxing the people so severely that

Old Testament History **Ezra 7-10; Nehemiah 1-13** **Week Thirteen**

they could no longer maintain their property (vv.1-5). Nehemiah took charge and rectified the problem (vv.6-13). Nehemiah then records how he (as governor) had not eaten the governor's allowance during the twelve years he had served (from the twentieth to the thirty-second year of King Artaxerxes I—vv.14-19). These passages also record the material sacrifices Nehemiah had made so the work might continue. How has the blessing of giving become a reality in your life (Acts 20:35)?

Fourth Day

Nehemiah 6 When everything had been rebuilt except the doors and gates, Sanballat, Tobiah, and Geshem sent messages to Nehemiah encouraging him to meet them at Chephirim (vv.1-2). They were planning to harm Nehemiah (v.2). Nehemiah refused (vv.3-4) even after Sanballat falsely accused him of seeking to become king of Judah (vv.5-9). Nehemiah then entered the house of Shemaiah who encouraged him to flee to the temple (v.10). Nehemiah refused (v.11), realizing that Tobiah and Sanballat had hired him to speak these things (v.12). They desired to have an evil report to discredit Nehemiah's character (vv.13-14), for no layman could enter those areas where only priests were allowed (Numbers 18:7). When the wall was almost completed Nehemiah's enemies unleashed their most deceptive tactics. We must never, never, forget this point as we fulfill God's calling on our lives.

The wall was completed in fifty-two days (v.15). When the enemies saw what had been accomplished, they lost their confidence and recognized that the work was done with the help of God (v.16). Even after the work was completed, Tobiah continued to send frightening letters to Nehemiah (vv.17-19).

Nehemiah 7 After the wall was completed, Nehemiah placed Hanani (his brother) and Hananiah ("the commander of the fortress") in charge of the city (vv.1-2). They were to open the gates only when the sun was hot, and guards were to be stationed throughout the city (v.3). The city was very large but short on inhabitants; the houses were not yet built (v.4).

Now that the wall was rebuilt, Nehemiah needed to organize the national life of the Jews. This chapter (from verse 5) is almost the same as Ezra 2, for it lists the people who had returned to Jerusalem with Zerubbabel and Jeshua (almost 100 years earlier). Since genealogies were of utmost importance to the Jews, Nehemiah realized this task needed special attention.

Read Nehemiah 8. Reference Point 58, *Ezra Reads the Law in Jerusalem and the Jews Repent*, is associated with this chapter.

1. In what location did the people gather (v.1)? What did the people ask of Ezra? In what day of what month did these events occur?

2. According to verses 2-12, how long did Ezra read from the Law? How did the people respond to what they heard? The phrase "translating to give the sense so that they understood the reading" (v.8) may refer not only to an exposition of the Law but also a translation of the Law from Hebrew into Aramaic.

Old Testament History   *Ezra 7-10; Nehemiah 1-13*   **Week Thirteen**

3. When Israel heard the Law (vv.13-18), what feast did they observe (for assistance read Leviticus 23:33-44)? In what month did these events occur (read Nehemiah 8:2)? Why was this particular feast was observed? How long had it been since booths were built during this feast?

Fifth Day

Read Nehemiah 9, which is associated with Reference Point 58.

1. On the twenty-fourth day of the month the nation confirmed the seriousness of their commitment to Jehovah (vv.1-3). What did they do to confirm their commitment?

2. Did you notice how familiar you were with the events reviewed in verses 5-37? Yes, the Lord has blessed the time you have invested in His word. What was the main thing you learned as you read these verses? Did you learn anything new about the price a nation pays for sin? If so, record what you learned below?

3. What did the nation do in verse 38? Whose names were on this document?

Read Nehemiah 10, which is associated with Reference Point 58.

1. The names of the people who signed the document (covenant) are listed in verses 1-27. The leaders of the nation, along with the priests and the Levites, signed this document. Their signing confirms what was stated in Nehemiah 9:38. What did the other Jews promise in verses 28-31?

2. They made another promise in verses 32-33. What was that and what was it for?

3. Write down at least three of the promises the people made in verses 34-39? From Israel's track record, do you think they will remain true to what they have promised? Just wait and see!

Nehemiah 11 The leaders of the Jews lived in Jerusalem, but lots were cast and one of ten Jewish men living outside Jerusalem was brought to live in the city (v.1). The remaining ninety percent lived in other cities (v.1). The people blessed all who voluntarily moved into Jerusalem (v.2). Those who lived in the city are listed in verses 3-24. Tallying all the numbers reveals that over 3,000 men lived in Jerusalem. If this number represented one-tenth of the total number of men living in Judah (v.1), the population had increased greatly since the return of Zerubbabel in Ezra 2:64-67 (these verses in Ezra represent a figure that includes men, women, and children). Note: Jerusalem, even with the wall completed, was not densely populated compared to the days of the kings. People may have been reluctant to live there because they would have had to build new homes and establish new businesses. Perhaps they were also concerned that living so close to the

Old Testament History   *Ezra 7-10; Nehemiah 1-13*   **Week Thirteen**

temple would require greater obedience to God's word.

Verses 25-36 list towns and villages in the territories of Judah (vv.25-30) and Benjamin (vv.31-36).

Sixth Day

<u>Nehemiah 12</u> Verses 1-9 list the priests and Levites who returned with Zerubbabel (the governor) and Jeshua (the high priest) in the book of Ezra. Verses 10-11 record Jeshua's descendants. Verses 12-21 list the sons of the priests named in verses 1-7 who lived in the days of Joiakim, Jeshua's successor, and verses 22-26 list the Levites in the day of Joiakim and afterwards.

The wall is dedicated in verses 27-43. Levites were summoned to Jerusalem to sing at this dedication (vv.27-29). The priests and Levites purified themselves, the people, the gates, and the wall (v.30). Nehemiah had two great choirs (as well as the people) walk along the top of the wall in different directions (vv.31-39). They met at the temple and sacrifices were offered with great joy (vv.40-43). "The joy of Jerusalem was heard from afar" (v.43). Wouldn't you have enjoyed being there?

Verses 44-47 describe how the needs of those who served in the temple were to be met.

<u>Nehemiah 13:1-3</u> The reading of the Law revealed that no Ammonite or Moabite was to enter the assembly of God (v.1, Deuteronomy 23:3-4). In other words, mixed marriages were strictly forbidden. When these words were heard, the Jews who had married foreign women were excluded from Israel. Pinpointing the timing of the events of verses 1-3 is hard. Some scholars place them before the dedication of the wall and others afterwards.

Nehemiah visited King Artaxerxes I (v.6), but during his absence Israel fell into sin. However, Nehemiah returned and guided the nation to obedience. You will discover how this occurred in verses 4-31. The prophet Malachi prophesied during this era.

Read Nehemiah 13:4-29, which is associated with Reference Point 59, *Nehemiah Discovers the Jews Have Sinned*.

1. The events of verses 4-9 occurred before the events of verses 1-3 ("Now prior to this"—v.4). What had Eliashib (the high priest) done during Nehemiah's absence (vv.4-9)? Don't let what is stated about King Artaxerxes I confuse you (v.6). He most definitely was King of Persia, but since Persia had overthrown Babylon, and since many Jews were still in Babylon, he is referred to as "Artaxerxes king of Babylon." Who was Tobiah, and to what nation did he belong (read Nehemiah 2:10)?

2. What did Nehemiah do to Tobiah's room in the courts of the temple? Can you believe Nehemiah's zeal? What causes a man to have such zeal?

3. What problem did Nehemiah resolve in verses 10-14 (a brief answer is sufficient)?

114

Old Testament History   *Ezra 7-10; Nehemiah 1-13*   *Week Thirteen*

4. What problem did Nehemiah eliminate in verses 15-22?

5. What problem did Nehemiah resolve in verses 23-29?

Read Nehemiah 13:30-31, which is associated with Reference Point 60, *Nehemiah Completes the Process of Cleansing the Jews*.

1. What did Nehemiah accomplish in verses 30-31? Can you believe Nehemiah would have to deal with such issues after all that the Lord had done for Israel? How can this serve as a warning to us?

You have now finished the History portion of the Old Testament and all 60 Reference Points. Congratulations! You have done a great job, and the Lord is thrilled with all you have learned. We hope you are pleased with your progress. 400 years of silence lies between these latest events in Nehemiah and the arrival of John the Baptist (in the New Testament), which means that all the books you have not yet studied in the Old Testament (Job through Malachi) fit somewhere between Reference Point 1 and Reference Point 60.

May our Lord bless you and allow the word of God to become your recreation, your pastime, your hobby, what you do on the weekends, but never your life. Only Christ Himself is our "Life" (Colossians 3:4). Walk on!

If you desire to continue your study of the Old Testament, prayerfully consider our Isaiah Commentary as a guide into the world of prophecy. Isaiah is the perfect launch pad for a look at the end times, the millennial reign of Christ, and a refreshing connection to the Jewish history you have just completed. A study of Isaiah exposes you to most all the Old Testament writing prophets, as well as Revelation. The commentary and teaching audios are available from our website, lifeonthehill.org.

History Course Reference Index

60 Old Testament Reference Points

General Map of Israel

Conquest of Land West of the Jordan (map)

The Approximate Territory the Twelve Tribes Possessed (map)

The Judges of Israel (plus blank)

The Journey of the Ark (map)

The Circuit of Samuel (map)

The Division of the Kingdom (map)

The Kings of Israel & Judah (timeline)

Kings of the Divided Kingdom, Israel (plus blank)

Kings of the Divided Kingdom, Judah (plus blank)

The Kings of Assyria

The Kings of Syria (Aram-Damascus)

The Kings of Neo-Babylonia

Chronology of the Persian Kings

Background Information for Ezra, Nehemiah, and Esther

Scan here with your phone camera for an additional free resource on the kings of the divided kingdom.

60 Old Testament Reference Points (1-20)

1 — Creation of the Heavens and Earth; Creation of Man
Genesis 1:1-2:25

2 — The Fall of Man and Resulting Curse
Genesis 3:1-24

3 — Cain Kills Abel, Cain Cursed; Seth Born
Genesis 4

4 — Noah and the Flood
Genesis 6-9

5 — Population of the Earth through Shem, Ham, and Japheth
Genesis 10:1-32

6 — The Tower of Babel
Genesis 11:1-9

7 — Abraham's Call
Genesis 11:26-12:9

8 — Ishmael is Born to Abraham and Hagar
Genesis 16:1-16

9 — Isaac is Born to Abraham and Sarah
Genesis 21:1-7

10 — God Calls Abraham to Offer Isaac as a Sacrifice
Genesis 22:1-19

11 — Isaac Marries Rebekah
Genesis 24:62-67

12 — Jacob and Esau are Born
Genesis 25:19-26

13 — Esau Sells His Birthright to Jacob
Genesis 25:27-34

14 — Jacob Leaves for Paddan-Aram
Genesis 28:1-5

15 — Jacob Marries Leah and Rachel
Genesis 29:1-30

16 — 11 of Jacob's Sons are Born
Genesis 29:31-30:24
(All 12 listed in Gen. 35:22-26)

17 — Jacob Wrestles with God; Jacob's Name Changed to Israel
Genesis 32:22-32

18 — Joseph (Jacob's Son) Sold into Egypt
Genesis 37:1-36

19 — Joseph Given Leadership Role in Egypt
Genesis 41:37-49

20 — Manassaeh and Ephraim Born to Joseph in Egypt
Genesis 41:50-52

60 Old Testament Reference Points (21-40)

21 — Jacob (Israel) Moves His Family to Egypt
Genesis 46:1-34

22 — Jacob Dies and is Buried; Joseph Dies
Genesis 49:33-50:26

23 — Israel Placed in Slavery in Egypt
Exodus 1:8-22

24 — Moses' Birth and Rearing in Egypt
Exodus 2:1-15

25 — God Calls Moses to Deliver Israel
Exodus 3:1-4:23

26 — Moses and Aaron Lead Israel Out of Egypt
Exodus 12:30-39

27 — Moses Leads Israel Through the Red Sea
Exodus 14:21-31

28 — Moses Receives the Law at Mount Sinai
Exodus 20:21-24:18

29 — At Mount Sinai, Moses Receives Instructions for the Tabernacle and the Priestly Service
Exodus 25-31

30 — Israel Builds Golden Calf and Moses Breaks Tablets of Stone
Exodus 32:1-29

31 — The Tabernacle is Set Up at Mount Sinai
Exodus 40:1-38

32 — Israel Moves from Mt. Sinai to Kadesh; 12 Spies Enter Canaan
Numbers 10:11-14:38

33 — Israel's Time in the Wilderness
Numbers 16-17

34 — Israel Returns to Kadesh
Numbers 20:1-21

35 — Israel Defeats the Amorites on the East Side of the Jordan
Num. 21:21-35

36 — Reuben, Gad, and Part of the Tribe of Manasseh Receive the Conquered Territory East of the Jordan
Numbers 32

37 — Moses Dies
Deuteronomy 34:1-8

38 — Joshua Leads Israel into Canaan and Takes Much of the Land
Joshua 1:1-12:24

39 — Canaan Divided Among the Remaining Tribes
Joshua 13:1-21:45

40 — Judges Rule After Joshua
Judges 1:1-21:25

60 Old Testament Reference Points (41-60)

41	42	43	44	45
Samuel Rules as Last Judge of Israel 1Samuel 7:3-17	**Saul Becomes First King of Israel** 1Samuel 10:1-27 1050 BC	**David Becomes Second King of Israel** 2Samuel 5:1-5 1010 BC	**God Promises David that One of His Descendants Will Sit on His Throne Forever; Jesus Will Fulfill this Prophecy** 1Chron. 17:10b-14	**David's Sin with Bathsheba** 2Samuel 11:1-27

46	47	48	49	50
David Overthrown by His Son Absalom 2Samuel 15:1-37	**David Regains the Throne** 2Samuel 19:1-43	**Solomon Rules as King over Israel and Judah** 1Kings 1:28-40 970 BC	**Solomon Builds the Temple** 1Kings 6:1-38	**Kingdom Splits into Israel (North) and Judah (South)** 1Kings 12:1-20 931 BC

51	52	53	54	55
The 19 Kings of the Northern Kingdom; First 12 Rulers of the Southern Kingdom 1Kings 12:21- 2Kings 17:5	**Assyria Takes the Northern Kingdom into Exile** 2Kings 17:6-41 722 BC	**Kings of the Southern Kingdom after Northern Kingdom's Exile** 2Kings 18:1-24:20	**Babylon, under Nebuchadnezzar, Destroys Jerusalem and Solomon's Temple; Southern Kingdom Exiled** 2Kings 25:1-21 586 BC	**Persia Overthrows Babylon** 2Chron. 36:20-23 536 BC

56	57	58	59	60
Persia Allows a Remnant of Jews to Return & Rebuild the Temple in Jerusalem Ezra 1:1-11	**Persia Allows Nehemiah to Rebuild the Wall Around Jerusalem** Nehemiah 2:1-8 445 BC	**Ezra Reads the Law in Jerusalem and the Jews Repent** Nehemiah 8-10	**Nehemiah Discovers the Jews Have Sinned** Nehemiah 13:4-29	**Nehemiah Completes the Process of Cleansing the Jews** Neh. 13:30-31

General Map of Israel

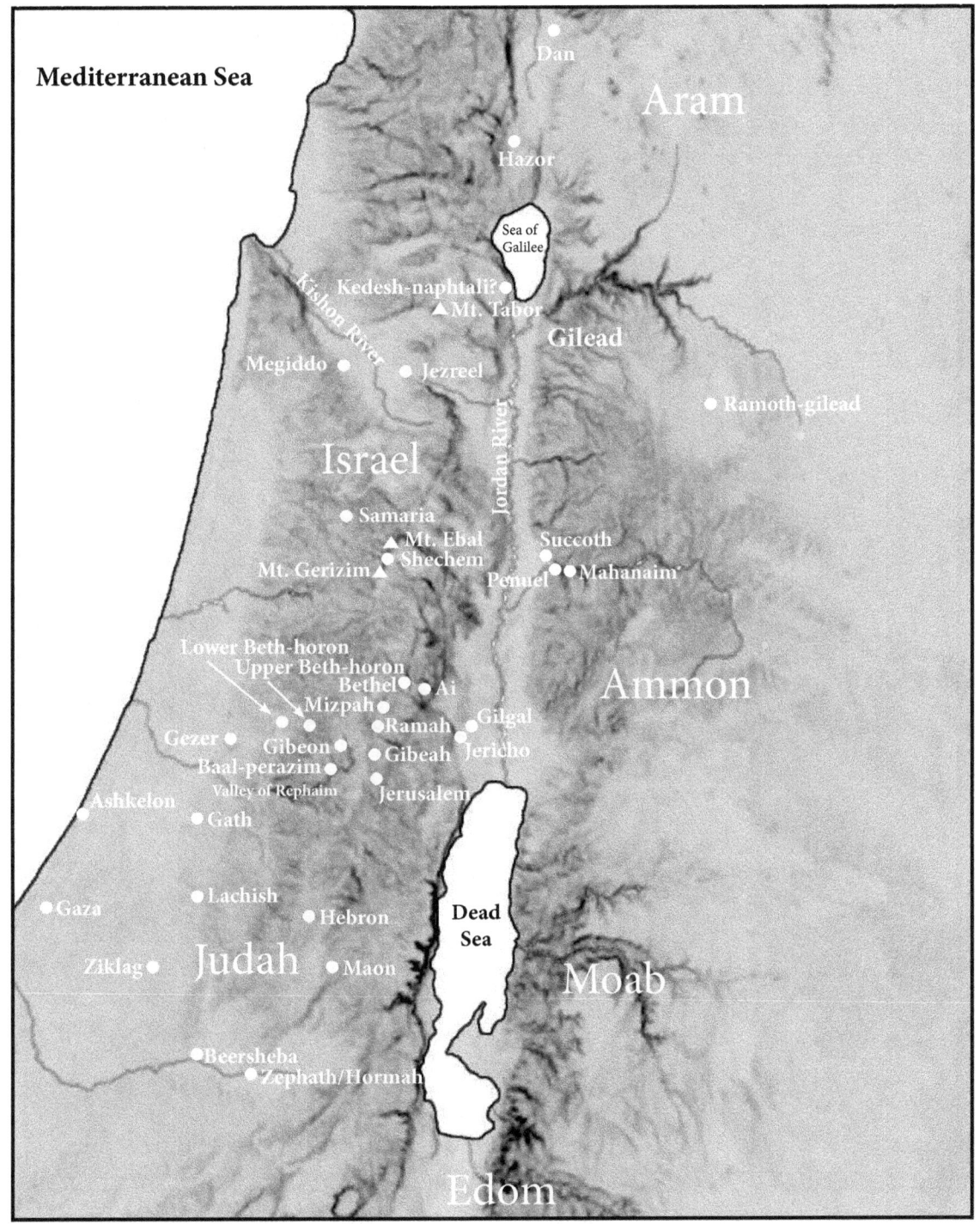

Conquest of The Land West of The Jordan

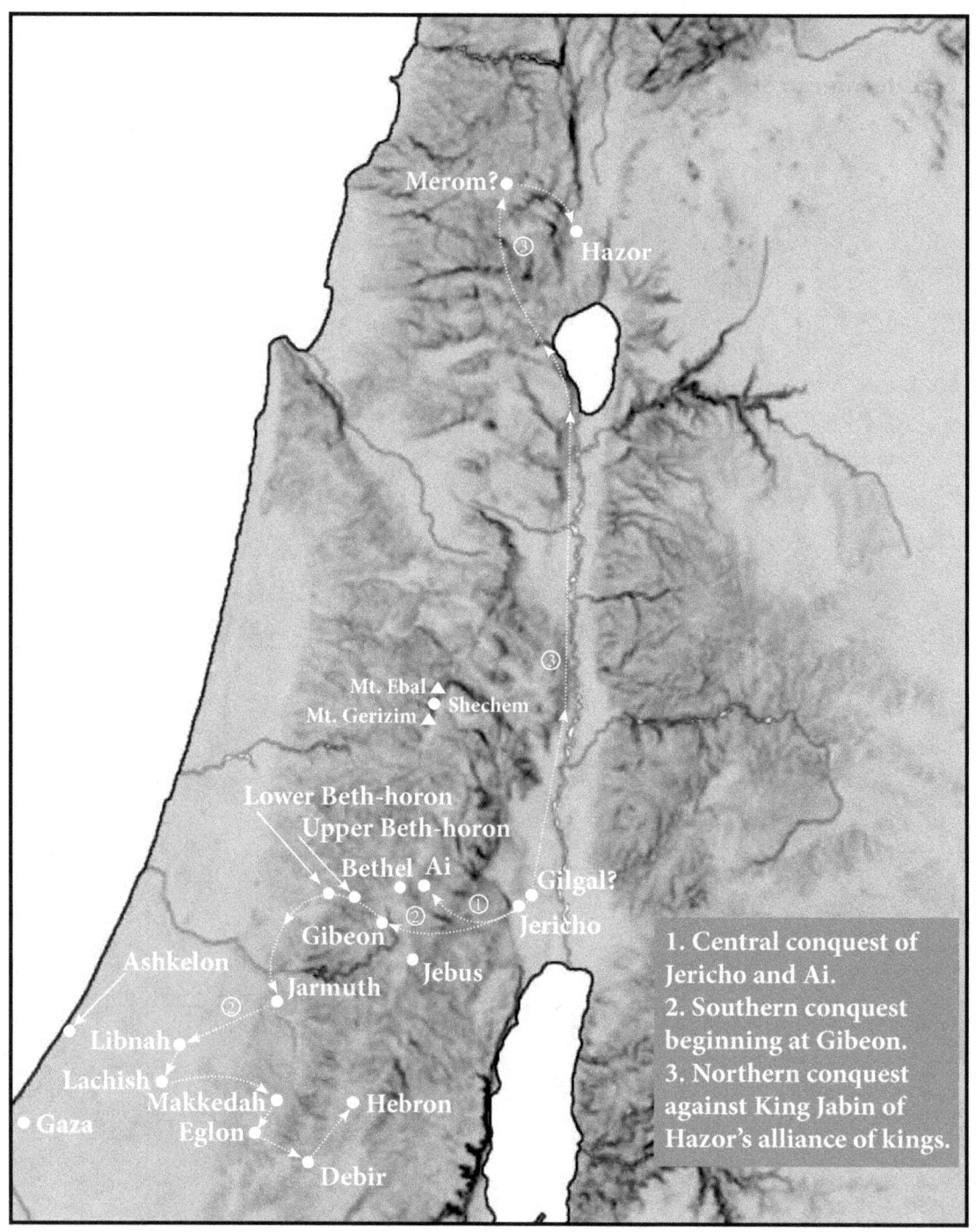

1. Central conquest of Jericho and Ai.
2. Southern conquest beginning at Gibeon.
3. Northern conquest against King Jabin of Hazor's alliance of kings.

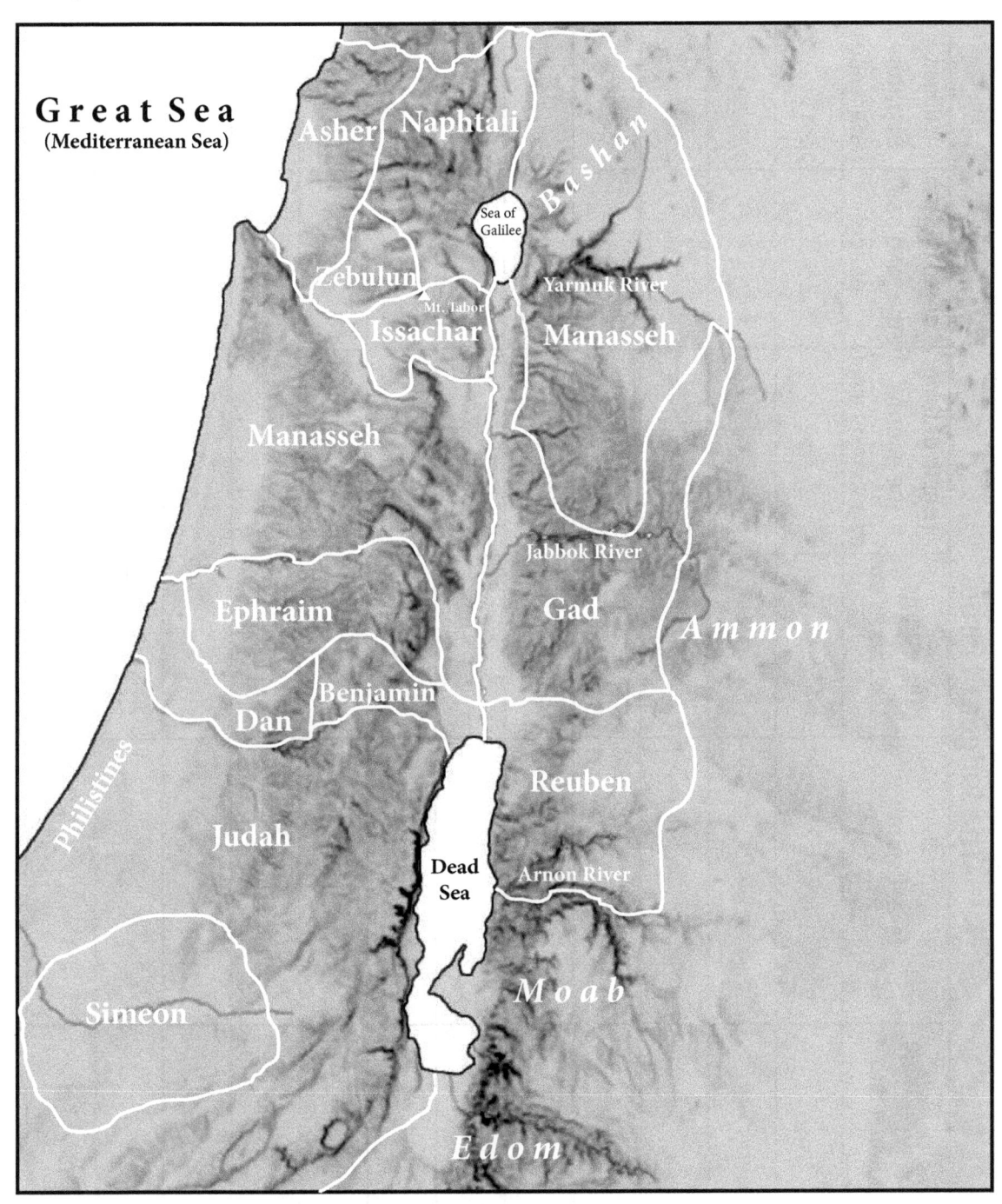

The Approximate Territory the Twelve Tribes Possessed

The Judges of Israel

The Judge that God raised up	Tribe the Judge belonged to	Israel's Sin	The enemy God raised up	Length of time the enemy oppressed Israel	Length of time the land had peace	Judges Scripture References
1.						3:9-11
2.						3:12-30
3.						3:31
4.						4:4-5:31
5.						6:11-8:35
6.						10:1-2
7.						10:3-5
8.						11:1-12:7
9.						12:8-10
10.						12:11-12
11.						12:13-15
12.						13:2-16:31

The Judges of Israel

The Judge that God raised up	Tribe the Judge belonged to	Israel's Sin	The enemy God raised up	Length of time the enemy oppressed Israel	Length of time the land had peace	Judges Scripture References
1. Othniel	Judah		Mesopotamians King Cushan	8	40	3:9-11
2. Ehud	Benjamin		Moabites King Eglon	18	80	3:12-30
3. Shamgar	Naphtali?		Philistines	?	?	3:31
4. Deborah	Ephraim		Canaanites King Jabin	20	40	4:4-5:31
5. Gideon	Manasseh		Midianites	7	40	6:11-8:35
6. Tola	Issachar				23	10:1-2
7. Jair	Gilead				22	10:3-5
8. Jephthah	Gilead		Ammonites	18	6	11:1-12:7
9. Ibzan	(Bethlehem)				7	12:8-10
10. Elon	Zebulun				10	12:11-12
11. Abdon	Ephraim				8	12:13-15
12. Samson	Dan		Philistines	40	20	13:2-16:31

The Journey of the Ark

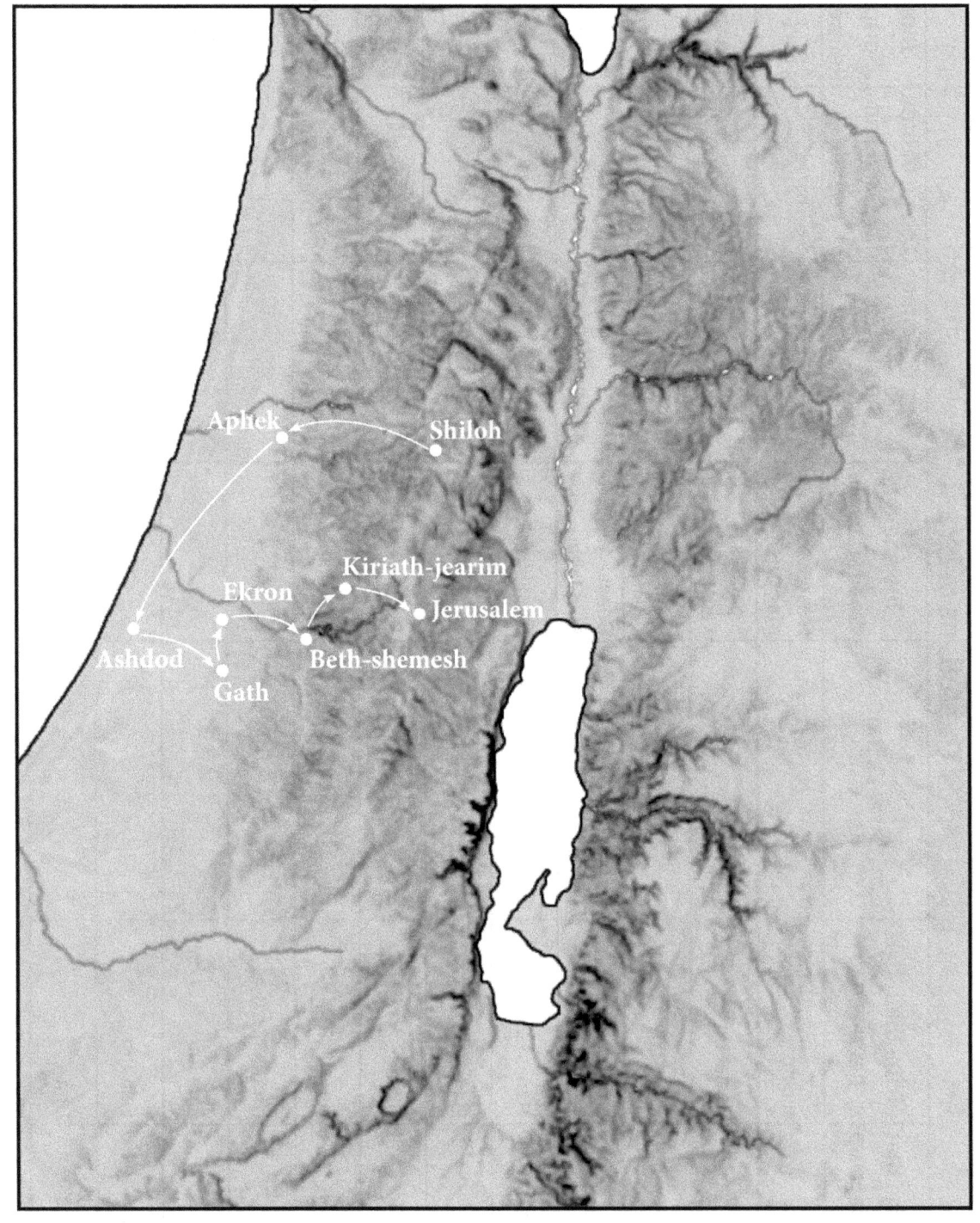

The Circuit of Samuel

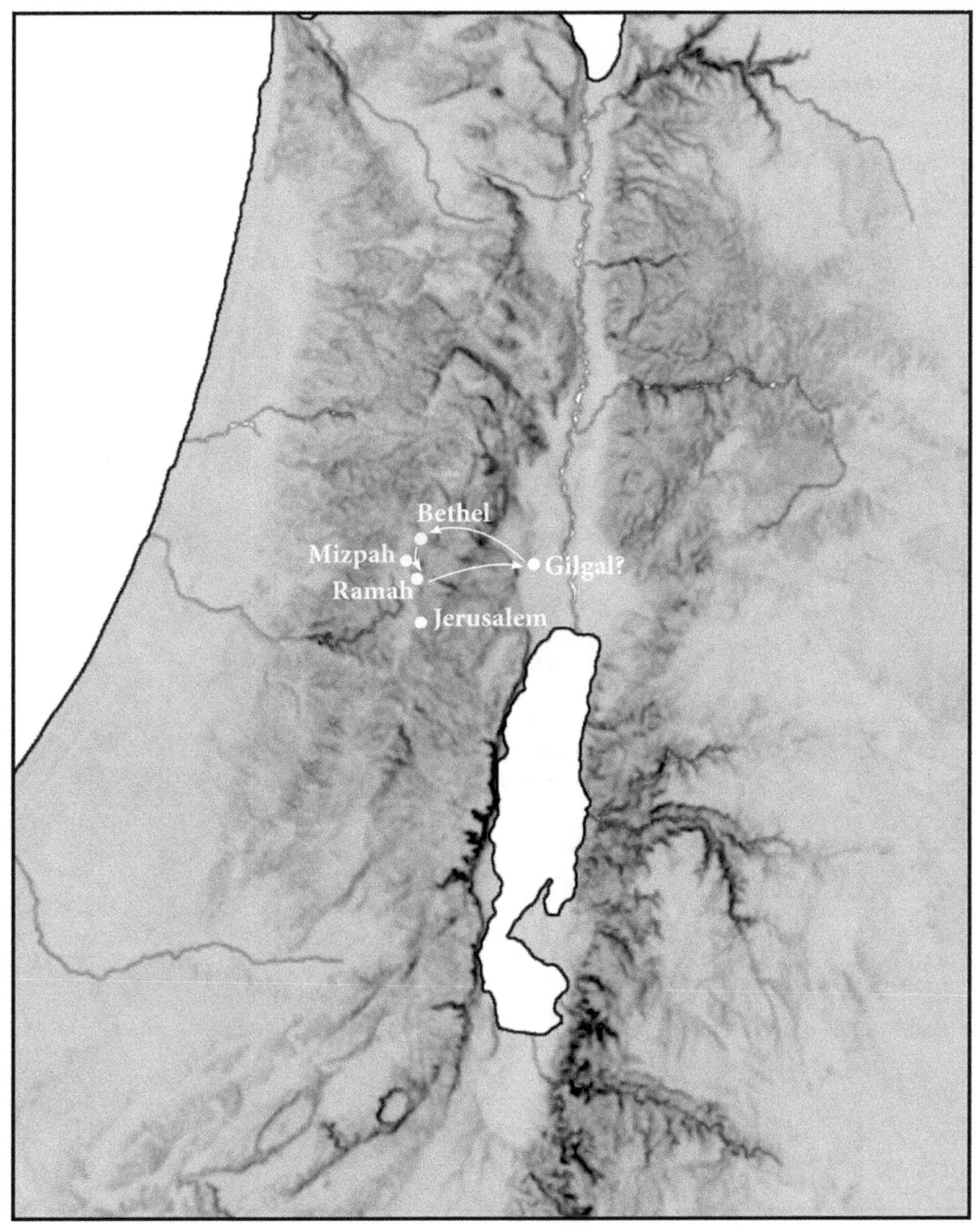

The Division of the Kingdom

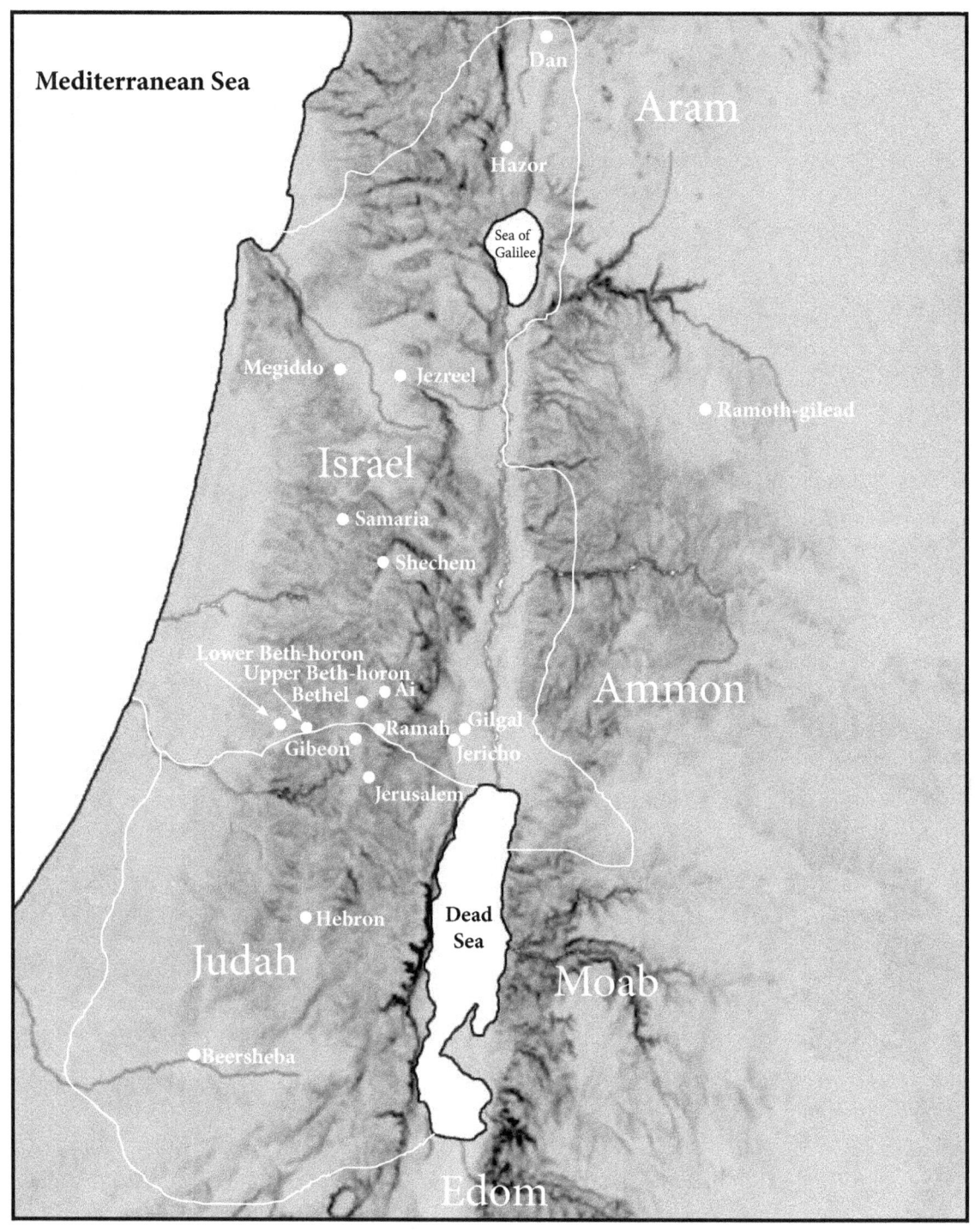

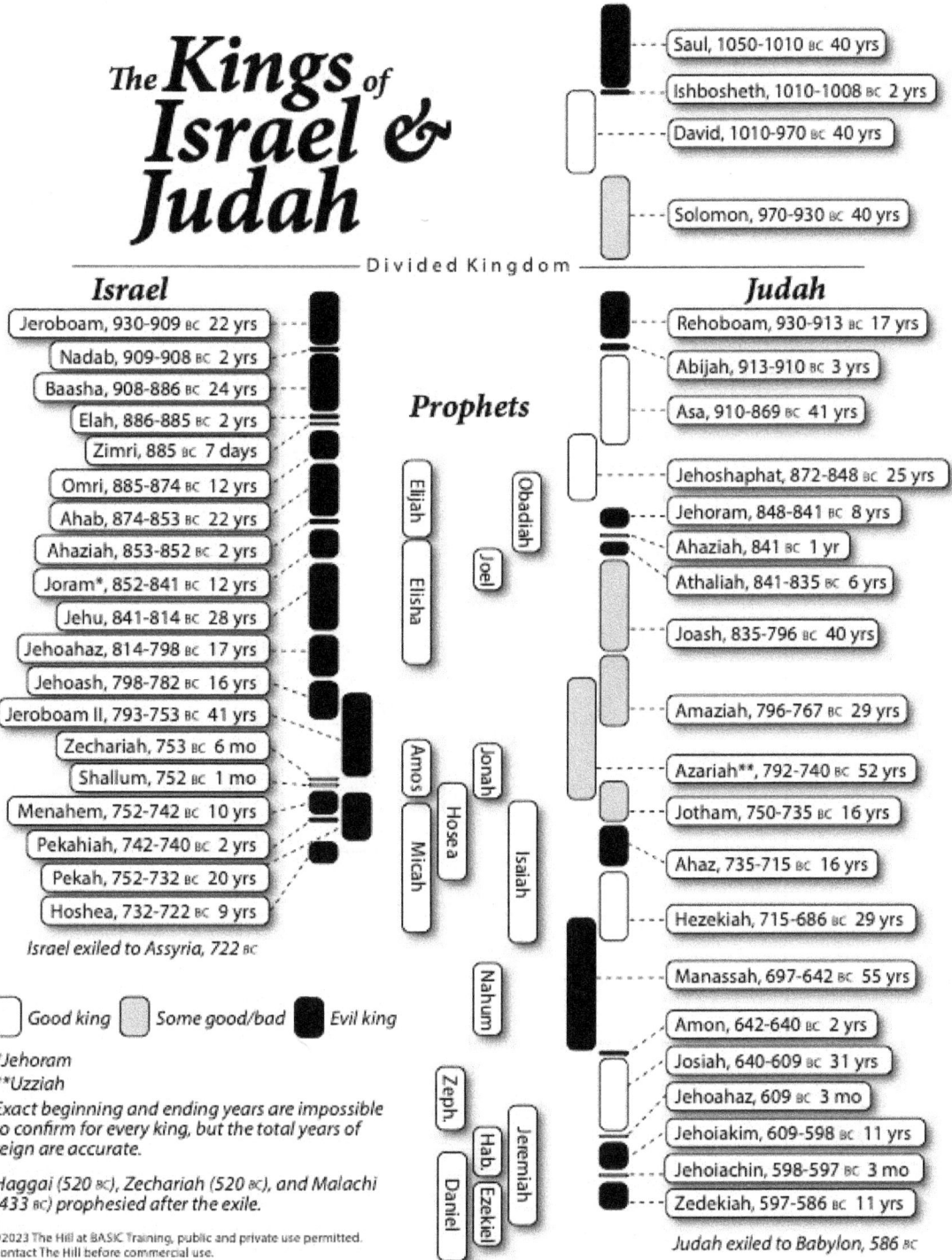

Kings of the Divided Kingdom: Israel				
Kings of Israel	Years of Reign	Character good/bad	Scripture References	Comments
1.			1Kings 11:26-14:20 2Chronicles 9:29-13:22	
2.			1Kings 15:25-28	
3.			1Kings 15:27-16:7 2Chronicles 16:1-6	
4.			1Kings 16:8-10	
5.			1Kings 16:10-20	
6.			1Kings 16:16-27	
7.			1Kings 16:28-22:40 2Chronicles 18:1-34	
8.			1Kings 22:40, 51-53 2Kings 1:1-17 2Chronicles 20:35-37	
9.			2Kings 3:1-3, 9:14-25 2Chronicles 22:5-7	
10.			2Kings 9:1-10:36 2Chronicles 22:7-12	
11.			2Kings 13:1-9	
12.			2Kings 13:10-25, 14:8-16 2Chronicles 25:17-24	
13.			2Kings 14:23-29	
14.			2Kings 15:8-12	
15.			2Kings 15:13-15	
16.			2Kings 15:16-22	
17.			2Kings 15:23-26	
18.			2Kings 15:27-31 2Chronicles 28:5-8	
19.			2Kings 17:1-41	

Kings of the Divided Kingdom: Israel

Kings of Israel	Years of Reign	Character good/bad	Scripture References	Comments
1. Jeroboam	22	Bad	1Kings 11:26-14:20 2Chronicles 9:29-13:22	
2. Nadab	2	Bad	1Kings 15:25-28	
3. Baasha	24	Bad	1Kings 15:27-16:7 2Chronicles 16:1-6	
4. Elah	2	Bad	1Kings 16:8-10	
5. Zimri	7 days	Bad	1Kings 16:10-20	
6. Omri	12	Very Bad	1Kings 16:16-27	
7. Ahab	22	Wicked	1Kings 16:28-22:40 2Chronicles 18:1-34	
8. Ahaziah	2	Bad	1Kings 22:40, 51-53 2Kings 1:1-17 2Chronicles 20:35-37	
9. Joram (Jehoram)	12	Bad	2Kings 3:1-3, 9:14-25 2Chronicles 22:5-7	
10. Jehu	28	Bad	2Kings 9:1-10:36 2Chronicles 22:7-12	
11. Jehoahaz	17	Bad	2Kings 13:1-9	
12. Jehoash	16	Bad	2Kings 13:10-25, 14:8-16 2Chronicles 25:17-24	
13. Jeroboam II	41	Bad	2Kings 14:23-29	
14. Zechariah	6 Mo	Bad	2Kings 15:8-12	
15. Shallum	1 Mo	Bad	2Kings 15:13-15	
16. Menahem	10	Bad	2Kings 15:16-22	
17. Pekahiah	2	Bad	2Kings 15:23-26	
18. Pekah	20	Bad	2Kings 15:27-31 2Chronicles 28:5-8	
19. Hoshea	9	Bad	2Kings 17:1-41	

Kings of the Divided Kingdom: Judah				
Kings of Judah	**Years of Reign**	**Character good/bad**	**Scripture References**	**Comments**
1.			1Kings 12:1-14:13 2Chronicles 10:1-12:16	
2.			1Kings 15:1-8 2Chronicles 13:1-22	
3.			1Kings 15:9-24 2Chronicles 14:1-16:14	
4.			1Kings 22:41-50 2Chronicles 17:1-20:37	
5.			2Kings 8:16-24 2Chronicles 21:1-20	
6.			2Kings 8:25-29, 9:27-29 2Chronicles 22:1-9	
7.			2Kings 8:25-28, 11:1-20 2Chronicles 22:1-23:21	
8.			2Kings 11:1-12:21 2Chronicles 22:10-24:27	
9.			2Kings 14:1-14 2Chronicles 25:1-28	
10.			2Kings 15:1-7 2Chronicles 26:1-23	
11.			2Kings 15:32-38 2Chronicles 27:1-9	
12.			2Kings 16:1-20 2Chronicles 28:1-27	
13.			2Kings 18:1-20:21 2Chronicles 29:1-32:33	
14.			2Kings 21:1-18 2Chronicles 33:1-20	
15.			2Kings 21:19-23 2Chronicles 33:21-25	
16.			2Kings 22:1-23:30 2Chronicles 34:1-35:27	
17.			2Kings 23:31-33 2Chronicles 36:1-4	
18.			2Kings 23:34-24:5 2Chronicles 36:5-7	
19.			2Kings 24:6-16 2Chronicles 36:8-10	
20.			2Kings 24:17-25:7 2Chronicles 36:11-21	

Kings of the Divided Kingdom: Judah				
Kings of Judah	**Years of Reign**	**Character good/bad**	**Scripture References**	**Comments**
1. Rehoboam	17	Bad	1Kings 12:1-14:13 2Chronicles 10:1-12:16	
2. Abijam	3	Bad	1Kings 15:1-8 2Chronicles 13:1-22	
3. Asa	41	Good	1Kings 15:9-24 2Chronicles 14:1-16:14	
4. Jehoshaphat	25	Good	1Kings 22:41-50 2Chronicles 17:1-20:37	
5. Jehoram (Joram)	8	Bad	2Kings 8:16-24 2Chronicles 21:1-20	
6. Ahaziah	1	Bad	2Kings 8:25-29, 9:27-29 2Chronicles 22:1-9	
7. Athaliah (Queen)	6	Bad	2Kings 8:25-28, 11:1-20 2Chronicles 22:1-23:21	
8. Joash	40	Good	2Kings 11:1-12:21 2Chronicles 22:10-24:27	
9. Amaziah	29	Good	2Kings 14:1-14 2Chronicles 25:1-28	
10. Uzziah (Azariah)	52	Good	2Kings 15:1-7 2Chronicles 26:1-23	
11. Jotham	16	Good	2Kings 15:32-38 2Chronicles 27:1-9	
12. Ahaz	16	Bad	2Kings 16:1-20 2Chronicles 28:1-27	
13. Hezekiah	29	Good	2Kings 18:1-20:21 2Chronicles 29:1-32:33	
14. Manasseh	55	Very Wicked	2Kings 21:1-18 2Chronicles 33:1-20	
15. Amon	2	Bad	2Kings 21:19-23 2Chronicles 33:21-25	
16. Josiah	31	Good	2Kings 22:1-23:30 2Chronicles 34:1-35:27	
17. Jehoahaz	3 Mo	Bad	2Kings 23:31-33 2Chronicles 36:1-4	
18. Jehoiakim	11	Bad	2Kings 23:34-24:5 2Chronicles 36:5-7	
19. Jehoiachin	3 Mo	Bad	2Kings 24:6-16 2Chronicles 36:8-10	
20. Zedekiah	11	Bad	2Kings 24:17-25:7 2Chronicles 36:11-21	

Kings of Assyria, 1363-609 BC			
King	Years of Reign	King	Years of Reign
Ashur-uballit 1	1363-1328 BC	Ashur-rabi 2	1012-972 BC
Enlil-nirari	1327-1318 BC	Ashur-resh-ishi 2	971-967 BC
Arik-den-ili	1317-1306 BC	Tiglath-Pileser 2	966-935 BC
Adad-nirari 1	1305-1274 BC	Ashur-dan 2	934-912 BC
Shalmaneser 1	1273-1244 BC	Adad-nirari 2	911-891 BC
Tukulti-Ninurta 1	1243-1207 BC	Tukulti-Ninurta 2	890-884 BC
Ashur-nadin-apli	1206-1203 BC	Ashurnasirpal 2	884-859 BC
Ashur-nirari 3	1202-1197 BC	Shalmaneser 3	859-824 BC
Enlil-kudurri-usur	1196-1192 BC	Shamshi-Adad 5	824-811 BC
Ninurta-apal-Ekur	1191-1179 BC	Adad-nirari 3	811-783 BC
Ashur-dan 1	1178-1133 BC	Shalmaneser 4	783-773 BC
Ninurta-tukulti-Ashur	1132 BC	Ashur-dan 3	773-755 BC
Nutakkil-Nusku	1132 BC	Ashur-nirari 5	755-745 BC
Ashur-resh-ishi 1	1132-1115 BC	Tiglath-Pileser 3	745-727 BC
Tiglath-Pileser 1	1114-1076 BC	Shalmaneser 5	727-722 BC
Asharid-apal-Ekur	1075-1074 BC	Sargon 2	722-705 BC
Ashur-bel-kala	1073-1056 BC	Sennacherib	705-681 BC
Eriba-Adad 2	1055-1054 BC	Esarhaddon	681-669 BC
Shamshi-Adad 4	1053-1050 BC	Ashurbanipal	669-631 BC
Ashurnasirpal 1	1049-1031 BC	Assur-etil-ilani	631-627 BC
Shalmaneser 2	1030-1019 BC	Sin-sar-iskun	627-612 BC
Ashur-nirari 4	1018-1013 BC	Assur-uballit 2	612-609 BC
		Fall of Nineveh	612 BC
		Fall of Haran	610 BC
		Fall of Carchemish	605 BC

Kings of Syria (Aram-Damascus)			
King	Dates of Reign	Scripture	Notes
Hezion	940-915 BC	1Kings 11:23-25, 15:18	
Tabrimmon	915-900 BC	1Kings 15:18	
Ben-hadad 1	900-860 BC	1Kings 15:18 & 20	
Ben-hadad 2	860-841 BC	1Kings 20	Also called Hadadezer
Hazael	841-806 BC	2Kings 8:15	
Ben-hadad 3	806-770 BC	2Kings 13:3	
Rezin	750-732 BC	2Kings 15:37	

Kings of Neo-Babylonia			
King	Dates of Reign	Scripture	Notes
Nabopolassar	625-605 BC	2Kings 23:29	
Nebuchadnezzar	605-562 BC	2Kings 24-25, Daniel 1-4, 2Chron. 36:6-13	Son of Nabopolassar
Amel-Marduk	562-560 BC	2Kings 25:27-30, Jer. 52:31-34	Son of Nebuchadnezzar, also called Evil-Merodach
Neriglissar	560-556 BC	Jer. 39:3 & 13	Son-in-law of Nebuchadnezzar
Labashi-Marduk	556 BC		Son of Neriglissar
Nabonidus	556-539 BC	(Belshazzar) Daniel 5:1-30	Son-in-law of Nebuchadnezzar, co-ruled with Nitocris and Belshazzar

Chronology of the Persian Kings

King	Dates of Reign	Bible Correlation	Greek Correlation
Cyrus	539-530 BC	Return of Zerubbabel and Jeshua (Ezra 1-3)	
Cambyses	530-522 BC	Rebuilding at Jerusalem ceased (Ezra 4)	
Darius 1	522-486 BC	Haggai & Zechariah prophesy (520 BC), Temple completed (516 BC, Ezra 5 & 6)	Greeks defeat Persians at Marathon (490 BC)
Xerxes	486-464 BC	Story of Esther (Esther 1-9)	Greeks defeat Persians at Thermopolae (480 BC) and Salamis (479 BC). Herodotus (485-425 BC)
Artaxerxes 1	464-423 BC	Return of Ezra (458 BC, Ezra 7-10), Return of Nehemiah (445 BC, Neh. 1-2), Prophecy of Malachi (433 BC)	Golden Age (461-431 BC), Pericles (460-429 BC), Athens rules.
Darius 2	423-404 BC	Biblical Silence	Peloponnesian Wars (431-404 BC), Athens falls (404 BC), Sparta rules.
Artaxerxes 2	404-359 BC		Socrates (470-399 BC), Plato (428-348 BC), Aristotle (384-322 BC)
Artaxerxes 3	359-338 BC		Philip 2 of Macedon defeats Greeks at Chaeronea (338 BC)
Arses	338-335 BC		
Darius 3	335-331 BC		Alexander the Great overthrows Persian Empire
Alexander	336-323 BC		Greek Empire Established

Background Information for Ezra, Nehemiah, and Esther

- Shortly after Persia overthrew Babylon in 536 BC (possibly as early as 539-538 BC), King Cyrus allowed many Jews to return to Jerusalem to rebuild the city as well as the temple (Ezra 1:1, Isaiah 44:28).
- The Jews who returned completed the temple in 516 BC (Ezra 6:15).
- Esther became queen of Persia in 479 BC (Esther 2:17).
- Esther (a Jew) saved the Jews in 473 BC (Esther 7-9).
- Ezra went to Jerusalem in 457 BC (Ezra 7:1 & 6).
- Nehemiah rebuilt the wall in Jerusalem in 445 BC, taking 52 days to complete the work (Nehemiah 6:15).

Five Persian kings ruled from 539 to 423 BC:

Cyrus	539-530 BC
Cambyses	530-522 BC
Darius 1	522-486 BC
Ahasuerus (Xerxes)	486-464 BC
Artaxerxes	464-423 BC
Darius 2	423-404 BC

King Cyrus of Persia allowed Zerubbabel and Jeshua (Joshua), along with a large remnant of Jews, to return to Jerusalem to begin rebuilding the temple and the city in 536 BC. These events are covered in Ezra 1-3. Note: There is ongoing debate over the year the Jews were allowed to return. Some think it was 536 BC while others believe it was 539-538 BC.

King Cambyses ruled in Persia when the work on the temple was delayed (Ezra 4:1-5 & 24).

King Darius 1 of Persia sent the decree (520 BC) that allowed the temple to be completed (Ezra 5-6). The temple was complete in 516 BC.

King Ahasuerus (Xerxes) followed Darius 1 and ruled Persia during the days of Esther (Esther 1:1). The story of Esther unfolds between chapter six and seven of Ezra (Esther 1-10).

King Artaxerxes is first addressed in Ezra 4:7-23. In verses 7-16, Rehum the commander, along with Shimshai the scribe, informed Artaxerxes that the Jews were rebuilding Jerusalem. Notice that the temple was not the issue here, for it had already been completed under the rule of Darius 1 in 516 BC. It was the city that was the concern (v. 16). Artaxerxes responded to Rehum, Shimshai, and their colleagues, telling them to issue a decree so the work on the city might cease (vv. 17-22). The work could be resumed only by means of a decree from King Artaxerxes (v. 21). In verse 23, the enemies of the Jews (Rehum, Shimshai, and their colleagues) stopped the work by force and evidently broke down part of the wall (Nehemiah 1:3-4). This probably occurred in 446 BC.

King Artaxerxes also allowed Ezra (the priest) to return in Ezra 7-10, and the spiritual condition of the nation was "rebuilt" under Ezra's leadership (around 457 BC). He also permitted Nehemiah to return to Jerusalem to rebuild the wall around the city in Nehemiah 2:1-8. This took place in 445 BC, sometime after the events of Ezra 4:7-23.

www.ingramcontent.com/pod-product-compliance
Lightning Source LLC
Chambersburg PA
CBHW081229170426